Blue Skies Guide

LANGKAWI

David Bowden

with contributions from
Nick Baker
Graeme Guy
David Hogan
Tom Reynolds

CONTENTS

Part 3 The Wildlife of Langkawi

Part 4 Travel Matters

Clockwise from top right: Teluk Datai; White-bellied Sea Eagle; nasi campur; outlying islands; sunset from Bon Ton Resort; Pantai Cenang; mangrove touring; Telaga Harbour

PART 1: INTRODUCTION

Aerial view Pelangi Beach Resort and Spa, the airport and Mount Machinchang

Langkawi's range of natural habitats, laid-back lifestyle and multiculturalism combine to make it an enchanting holiday island destination in Malaysia. The diverse landscape, with its multitude of animals and plants, provides travellers with a natural and tranquil alternative to the more visited islands in the region.

Ten Essential Langkawi Experiences

Langkawi has many things to see, places to explore, cultures to experience and people to meet. Narrowing down these experiences to ten is difficult, but here are those that make travelling to Langkawi so unique.

Foraging Around Local Markets

The Sunday markets in Padang Matsirat extend from late afternoon into early evening, and while they appeal to tourists, they are very much for the locals to stock up on fresh ingredients, socialize and buy their hawker-stall favourites. Known as a *pasar malam*, the night markets are vibrant and lively, with lots of treats and great photo opportunities.

Tempting treats at night markets

Watersports at Tanjung Rhu

Experiencing Thrilling Watersports

There's an extensive range of both passive and active watersports. Parasailing high above the water, pulled by a speedboat, offers a thrilling perspective on the coastline. There are four marinas with sailing, providing options from half-day cruises to extended expeditions into the islands of southern Thailand.

Zipping Through the Rainforest Canopy

Langkawi supports extensive stands of lowland tropical rainforest. An exciting way to appreciate the many forest features is to zipline through the rainforest canopy. There are several zipline operators on the island.

Thrilling rainforest canopy adventure

Pantai Cenang sunsets are spectacular

Sailing into a Setting Sun

Several operators offer cruises across the waters of the Andaman Sea surrounding Langkawi. A sunset cruise is great for experiencing the fresh air while being whisked from island to island by the forces of monsoon winds. Enjoy fine food, cool beverages, the chance to swim in remote waters and opportunities to photograph the setting sun.

Exploring Coastal Mangrove Forests

Large parts of coastal Langkawi are protected by thick mangrove forest. Take a small-boat journey to discover limestone caves, the unique aerial roots of the mangroves, and the animals, such as waterbirds, reptiles and monkeys, which live in the mangroves.

Explore mangroves in a kayak

Aerial adventures on Mount Machinchang

Temurun Waterfall

Admiring Cascading Waterfalls

There are several waterfalls on the main island, with Telaga Tujuh (Seven Wells) one of the most accessible despite a steep climb – rewarded with a swim in cool mountain pools deep in the forest.

Riding the Cable Car to Gunung Machinchang

One of the world's steepest cable cars provides access to Gunung Machinchang at 850m (2,789ft). Journey high above the rainforest canopy. The views from the summit are spectacular and extend off to Tarutao Island in neighbouring southern Thailand.

Wild Nature Walks

Several experienced nature guides on Langkawi are more than happy to share their locale with those who accompany them on a general nature trek, cruise or birdwatching walk.

Join a jungle trek

Island Hopping

While just four islands in the 99-island archipelago are developed, boat operators

Visit some of Langkawi's 99 islands

offer island-hopping excursions to islands like Dayung Bunting, which has a suspended freshwater lake.

Cycling Past Rice Padis

Join a cycling tour through the rice *padis* (or paddies) that are found on some of the island's lowlands. While rice is a staple for the islanders, the *padi* fields are also home to wildlife such as waterbirds and waders.

Explore the backroads on a bicycle

Langkawi is an archipelago of 99 islands. Perhaps confusingly, the main island is also called Langkawi, and is the island where almost all development is concentrated. The archipelago is situated within the Malaysian state of Kedah, and the mainland ports of Kuala Perlis (in the state of Perlis) and Kuala Kedah (in the state of Kedah) are the main departure points for regular ferry services from the mainland to Langkawi.

While many locals still farm the land and fish the sea, tourism and related service activities are now the biggest employers on the island. As is the case for many other resort islands in the region, visitors from around the globe travel here to enjoy the year-round warm weather, learn more about the culture, dine on delicious food and relax in one of many luxurious resorts.

Langkawi is blessed with expansive areas of natural vegetation over much of the islands, and unlike many other regional island resort destinations, its natural assets remain largely untouched. The fact that only four of the islands in the archipelago have any development is also an important point of difference. It means that the bulk of the islands and the ecosystems that they support remain as they have for millions of years. The flora and fauna that thrive here are as they have been for eons, yet they are accessible for visitors to explore.

Langkawi is covered by 60 per cent forest, 20 per cent agricultural land and 20 per cent developed areas. The topography varies from the flat coastal plains of Pantai Cenang to the mountainous peaks of Gunung Raya and Gunung Machinchang. There are many sandy beaches on the main island, and numerous deserted beaches on the other islands within the archipelago.

Tourism development is ongoing but is restricted to certain areas, so that the bulk of the archipelago remains untouched and the traditional values of the people are unaffected by it. Langkawi is now branded 'Naturally Langkawi' to promote it as a natural haven and choice for visitors. Some development has created localized environmental concerns, but checks and balances are in place to keep most of these issues under control. Concerned locals also work towards maintaining the delicate balance between sustaining the ecology and allowing development.

Many locals are involved in fishing

Geography and Environment

The islands of Langkawi are situated 50km (31 miles) off the mainland. The archipelago is very close to the maritime border with Thailand to the north, and immediately to the west, across the Andaman Sea, is the Indonesian island of Sumatra. The Malaysian island and state of Penang is situated 110km (68 miles) to the south of Langkawi. Langkawi has the map coordinates of 6° 21'N and 99° 48'E.

Langkawi covers an area of 478km^2 (185mi^2), with the main island measuring approximately 20km by 30km (12 by 19 miles). Two peaks (known as *gunung* in Bahasa Malaysia) dominate the main island, with Gunung Raya being the highest at 881m (2,890ft) and Gunung Machinchang at 701m (2,300ft). Other islands are so low that they disappear during the high tide, sometimes leading to confusion about how many islands there actually are in the group (some references suggest 103 islands, but it is generally accepted that there are only 99). The main island is 300km^2 (116mi^2). In comparison, Singapore is 712km^2 (274mi^2) and Penang 1,048km^2 (405mi^2).

Natural Paradise

In addition to having a good tourism infrastructure, including an international airport and cruise-ship terminal, much of Langkawi's natural vegetation remains intact. Rainforests and mangroves are the dominant plant communities, while coral reefs surround some of the islands. Even on the main island, where most of Langkawi's 70,000 residents live, there is still a sense of being close to nature. While developers would love to make a bigger mark on the skyline, few buildings are higher than the many coconut palms that thrive along island fringes.

Various ecosystems are protected as a UNESCO World Geopark. Langkawi has a fascinating geological history and has been recognized by UNESCO as a Geopark. It is this geodiversity and the biodiversity that thrives in the natural areas that has captured the attention of the scientific community and many visitors.

What is Geopark?

A Geopark is a defined area that ensures the sustainable protection of its geological formations and scientific assets. The United Nations Educational, Scientific and Cultural Organization (UNESCO) established a network of Geoparks, and in 2007 Langkawi became the first such park identified in the region. Some of the parks promote the awareness of geological hazards such as earthquakes, volcanoes and tsunamis, and experts and local authorities work with local communities to sustainably manage these areas. Management plans encourage economic benefits to local communities, with ecotourism an important industry in Langkawi. Mangrove tours through the coastal forests are one of the main tourist attractions in Langkawi.

There are currently some 60 Geoparks in eight Asian countries including 39 in China alone. These include several popular tourist sites, such as Mount Batur (Bali), Mount Rinjani (Lombok), Satun (Thailand), Jeju Island (South Korea), Dong Van Karst Plateau (Vietnam) and Dunhuang (China).

Climate

The island's climate is classified as equatorial, which means that it is typically warm and wet throughout most of the year. However, Langkawi does have a distinct dry season (December–March). Temperatures range from 22° C to 34° C, with humidity levels at 80–90 per cent. The climate is dominated by the monsoon (the movement of winds, which result from the differences in temperature over the sea and land), with most rain falling in April–August. Unlike countries that experience four seasons a year, tropical islands such as Langkawi only have a wet and a dry season.

In the region, the north-east monsoon delivers rain in November–March and the south-west monsoon brings rain in May–October. Most rain falls in Langkawi during the south-west monsoon, with the dry season being from December–March, when it is a good time to visit the island.

In December 2004, the word tsunami entered most people's vocabulary when disastrous waves wreaked havoc throughout several nations lining the Indian Ocean. An estimated 228,000 people lost their lives when an undersea megathrust earthquake of magnitude 9.1 to 9.3, with its epicentre on the west coast of northern Sumatra (Indonesia), resulted in waves of up to 30m (100ft). The tsunami destroyed many coastal communities in Indonesia, Thailand, Sri Lanka, India and several other nations, including Malaysia. The release of energy was reportedly the equivalent to 1,500 times that generated by the atomic bomb dropped on Hiroshima during the Second World War.

Bandar Aceh in Sumatra was the place worst affected by the tsunami. Langkawi,

The long golden beaches are a big draw

500km (310 miles) to the east, was mostly protected by the island of Sumatra, but Malaysia (Penang, Langkawi and parts of the Kedah coast) was affected and 67 deaths were attributed to the tsunami. Fishing boats, coastal houses, yachts and some coastal resorts were damaged. Today, early-warning tsunami systems are in place and most coastal resorts have a tsunami evacuation plan and warning signs in place.

Experts maintain that the mangroves lining coastal islands such as Langkawi were crucial in minimizing damage when the tsunami struck. The Food and Agricultural Organization (FAO) has noted that extensive areas of mangroves can reduce the loss of life and damage caused by tsunamis by taking the first brunt of the impact and by dissipating the energy of the wave as it passes through the mangroves.

Climatic Adaptions

Traditional island homes were built (and still are to some extent) to temper the outside weather. Early Malay village homes were built of locally sourced woven bamboo walls and roofing made from thatch (*atap*). Houses are built on stilts to keep floodwaters and wild animals at bay, while allowing the circulation of air to ensure that the house interior remains cool (cracks in the floor are intentional to enable this to happen).

Atap roofing, made from the fronds of Nipa, Bertam or Rumbia Palms, is a lightweight and excellent thermal insulator, which absorbs little heat during the day and cools quickly in the evening. Some houses still have *atap* roofs but most modern homes incorporate sheets of corrugated (galvanized) iron or tiles, which also reflect the heat. Screens in the gables allow hot air inside a house to escape.

Shutters were used to keep the light and heat out – they would be closed or drawn by day, and opened during the cooler times. Overhanging eaves minimized the direct effects of sunlight and heat. Many modern houses and buildings do not incorporate these elements and are more dependent on air conditioning to keep them habitable.

Visitors to Langkawi can see traditional homes in several villages around the island. An alternative is to visit small resorts such as Bon Ton, which is a collection of eight traditional houses from Langkawi that were relocated to their new resort home. These include houses up to 120 years old, including one with a *serambi* – an open, airy area attached to the main house where guests were entertained.

History

Geological History

Langkawi's geological history is fascinating and was the reason why various parts of the island were listed as a Geopark in 2007 (p. 11). The rocks of Langkawi are among the region's oldest strata, with the earliest sedimentary rocks dated by geologists to the Palaeozoic Era (541–251 million years ago, from the Cambrian to the Permian Period).

Langkawi's geology is the result of a long depositional history followed by tectonic and magmatic events, then by erosional forces that are ongoing. The first era took place alongside the margin of Gondwanaland (the supercontinent dating back 500 million years ago, the remnants of which comprise present-day South America, Antarctica, Australia, Africa, India and Arabia).

The geology is divided into four sedimentary formations and one granite formation. The latter intruded on the older sedimentary formations and, in parts, turned them into contact metamorphic rocks (marble, for example). Sedimentary rocks such as sandstone, conglomerate, shale, limestone, siltstone and mudstone are found on Langkawi. Gunung Raya is a granite outcrop that resulted from volcanic activity.

Surface and underground rock weathering began in the Jurassic Period, 200 million years ago, and is ongoing today. Langkawi's karst topography and geological formations are typical of limestone as it erodes. Karst is named after a location on the Dalmatian Coast in south-west Slovenia. The most striking features of this geology are the towering

Bujang Valley archaeological site

limestone cliffs, caves and underground drainage formed by millions of years of erosion. The soils that form on the limestone host many unique plant forms.

Human History

The state of Kedah has a fascinating history as it has been influenced by the Sumatran kingdom of Srivijaya, the Cola kingdom of South India, China, Siam (present-day Thailand) and Britain before Malaysia's independence in 1957.

Early History

Malaysia's earliest inhabitants were the Orang Asli, whose presence dates back thousands of years. Some still pursue a semi-nomadic existence in the rainforests of the peninsula. Kedah has been on sailing routes between the east and west for more than 1,500 years, when traders from Persia (now Iran), Arabia, southern India and parts of Africa set sail on the monsoon winds, crossing the Indian Ocean for Asia and back on reverse winds (the winds blow in an easterly direction in June–November and in the reverse direction in December–May).

Explorers from northern China appreciated the significance of the Straits of Malacca as a link between the Pacific and Indian Oceans. Admiral Cheng Ho, a Chinese naval admiral and envoy of the Chinese Emperor, recorded Langkawi in his logbook in 1405.

Strategically located at latitude 50° N, Kedah was where mariners first touched Asia from ports in northeastern Africa (10° N), the southern Arabian Peninsula (15° N) and southern India (7° N). Various coastal ports in Kedah became entrepôts or trading ports for the import of exotic products, as well as for the export of goods from Malaysia and the region. Early mariners traded glassware, cotton, camphor, sandalwood, forest products and ivory. With the goods came new ideas, philosophies and religions. There is every possibility that some of these vessels moored in the protective waters of Langkawi.

At this time, a Hindu-Buddhist society developed in the Lenggong Valley in southern Kedah and became one of the region's most important kingdoms. It was recognized as Malaysia's fourth UNESCO site in 2012, and the Bujang Valley Archaeological Museum 5km (3 miles) north of Sungai Petani is accessible to visitors. However, concerns have been expressed that parts of the UNESCO site are poorly maintained, so it may be best to contact the museum before venturing to the site.

Malaysian archaeologists from Universiti Sains Malaysia in Penang have been digging at various sites in Kedah for years. They have uncovered charcoal and artefacts dating back to the Neolithic Stone Age (2,500 years ago) at Sungai Batu just north of Sungai Petani. Modern technology has enabled the archaeologists to appreciate that what is known as the Kedah Tua kingdom was once on the coastline (it is now 8km/5 miles inland); industrial remains have been found here. The location enabled the iron forged here to be exported to many parts of the region, making it a very important Neolithic industrial site. The academic community is eager for the site to become part of the UNESCO-listed precinct. As a frame of reference, the famous three archaeological sites of Angkor, Bagan and Borobudur only date back 1,200 years.

Sungai Petani Neolithic site

Islam was introduced into Kedah by Indian and Arab traders almost 1,000 years ago.

Colonial Times

By the fifteenth century, the Straits of Malacca between Sumatra and Peninsular Malaysia's western coastline were regularly visited by mariners and traders. This vital shipping link connected China and the Spice Islands (Indonesia) with India, Africa and Arabia. Langkawi was strategically located at the northernmost extremity of the straits. By this time, the town of Melaka (Malacca) on Malaysia's mainland had become one of the region's most important ports.

Many legends and stories are associated with the history of Langkawi. Several locations echo with stories from the past, some strange and some tragic. A few are celebrated in specific locations, and whether or not a legend is believable appears unimportant to local visitors. Mahsuri's Curse is the most famous legend. It involves a beautiful young princess and bride named Mahsuri, who committed adultery and received the death sentence in 1829. With her dying breath, she cursed Langkawi's prosperity for seven generations, and many locals attribute any misfortune to this curse.

Many of the sheltered bays and the maze of mangroves provided protective shelter for pirates who once plundered unsuspecting ships sailing across the Andaman Sea.

Recent Developments

While Penang thrived as a major regional port, Langkawi remained very much a backwater until the then prime minister, Tun Dr Mahathir Mohamad, decided in 1986 to transform the islands within the state where he was born into a premier tourist destination. In 1987, the island was granted duty-free status. Langkawi Development Authority (LADA) was established to oversee the implementation of essential tourism infrastructure. Hotel and resort development soon followed.

Efforts have been made for this development to be sympathetic to the island's natural surroundings and there has been an unwritten understanding that the height of buildings should be limited. However, times are changing and a few tall buildings now dot the horizon but they are not as obvious as they are on other most resort islands in the region. Langkawi remains unique in that large areas are protected as natural habitats.

LADA office in Kuah

The People

Langkawi is mostly a community of small-scale rice farmers, rubber-estate workers, fishing people and traders whose ancestors have inhabited the islands for generations. Tourism is a growing industry that has developed over the past 25 years.

Life on the island moves at an unhurried pace and is very different from that on most other major regional tourist islands like Bali, Koh Samui and Phuket. Langkawi has attained a balance between maintaining traditional life and protecting the environment while incorporating modern infrastructure – simplicity and style coexist. Apart from the principal town of Kuah and the tourism development along a few of the main beaches (known as *pantai*), the other settlements on the islands are mostly small villages, or *kampungs*, as they are referred to in rural Malaysia. The main island, together with Tuba, Rebak and Dayang Bunting Islands, are the only ones with any development.

People living on the islands are mostly open and interested in outsiders, and visitors can expect a warm and friendly welcome. However, with more than 70 per cent of the population being Muslim, the islanders are conservative and visitors need to be respectful of their local customs, traditions and values. For example, while most visitors stay in resorts where Western bathing attire is the norm, many locals, especially females, bathe fully clothed when on public beaches. In such situations, visitors should cover themselves more than they would in a resort pool.

Many locals are employed in tourism

Artist creating a batik *masterpiece*

and hospitality and their command of English is good, although among themselves they converse mostly in Bahasa Malaysia. With visitors, they often speak 'Manglish' – mangled English or English with a local flavour. The islanders are justifiably proud of their achievements in transforming the island from a remote backwater just a few decades ago to the globally recognized tropical resort island that it is today.

Like most Malaysians, the residents of Langkawi love food and are delighted when visitors sample some of the fiery dishes on offer. They are always happy to recommend specific dishes and ingredients, and to direct visitors to their favourite hawker stall.

Padi Rice Farmers

Rice is one of the staples for all Malaysians, and it is grown on extensive areas of flat land in Langkawi. While palm oil and rubber are the dominant cash crops, rice is Malaysia's main food crop. This edible, starchy cereal was first cultivated in China about 4,500 years ago and is now the most important crop in the world, feeding more than half its population. It was first planted in Malaysia centuries ago, in Kedah's fertile Bujang Valley. Decades ago, canals and dams provided a controlled water supply, which helped farmers to plant two crops annually on the Kedah mainland. Kedah is Malaysia's 'rice bowl', with some 50 per cent of the nation's rice grown here.

Before modern rice-growing techniques were developed, farmers were dependent on natural cycles to grow their crop. They observed specific characteristics of their livestock, since animals are sensitive to changes in the weather. Restlessness among them indicated that the April rainy season was approaching and it was time to prepare the next rice crop. After a month of soaking rains, seeds were germinated, then often sown in a nursery in a small section of the *padi* field. Meanwhile the land was tilled, ploughed and conditioned. A month later the seedlings were planted throughout the field, and for the following 44 days the farmer kept pests at bay and the water levels up in the field. When the crop ripened between the end of October and mid-November, it was harvested by hand using sickles. Rice was threshed to separate the grains before being stored.

Technological advances have changed the rice-growing cycle, with two crops being grown in many parts of Malaysia. Meanwhile, the government is helping farmers grow more glutinous rice (*padi pulut*) in Langkawi, as market prices are higher for this than for ordinary rice. Some 1,729ha (4,272 acres) of single-crop, rain-fed rice is grown on Langkawi. While some rice is grown organically, the bulk of it is now dependent on a growing regime of weedicides, pesticides and compound fertilizers. Through run-off, small amounts of these products flow into the waters surrounding Langkawi. However, some farmers still introduce fish and ducks to their fields to control pests.

Visitors can learn more about the importance of rice at Laman Padi (the rice museum), see page 31. In the right season, they can get out in a *padi* and learn how to plant rice or how to harvest it.

Rice planting

Fishing Folk

Most of the fishing in the waters around Langkawi is of a modest scale, with small fishing boats best seen moored in protected mangrove-lined streams near Kuala Teriang, just north of the airport, or just off the village near Pantai Pasir Hitam (Black Sand Beach). The boats set to sea when the waters are not rough.

There are several fish farms (aquaculture) in the waters of Langkawi, including around Langgun, Simpang Tiga and Tuba Islands. Typically, these farms raise several types of fish in offshore cages, including various groupers, snappers, trevally and barramundi. Some fish farms are included in mangrove tours departing from the Kilim Jetty.

Anchovies are one of the fish caught in Langkawi waters. These tiny fish are eagerly consumed by Malaysians, especially when dried and served on top of a popular Malaysian breakfast dish, *nasi lemak*. Other fish, prawns, crabs and lobsters are also fished, and tuna boats set out to sea into the Indian Ocean, with

Visiting a fish farm

processing facilities located in Langkawi and Kuala Kedah. Sea-cucumber products, or *gamat*, are sold on Langkawi, but most of these are imported to the islands.

While the fishing industry is based on the sustainable harvesting of natural resources, some concerns have been expressed about commercial squid fishing at night using high-powered spotlights. The Malaysian conservation organization Sahabat Alam Malaysia has called for a ban on such lights, suggesting that other species and juvenile squid also get caught, affecting the sustainability of the industry. Concerns have also been expressed about the water quality, especially around the main island. Agricultural run-off, leachate from waste dumps and sewerage treatment on the island are causing localized pollution.

Small-scale squid jigging is a popular activity with some visitors, especially during the season in November–April, and around Pulau Dayang Bunting and Pulau Singha Besar. It requires a special lure and a skilful jerking motion to catch a squid.

Fishing fleet at Kuala Teriang

Rubber Tappers

Most Malaysians of Indian heritage live near the rubber plantations on the eastern side of the island around Kisap. They came to Malaya from India when the British ruled both. Most were Hindu Tamils and arrived as labourers to work in estates.

Hevea brasiliensus (rubber) is a tropical rainforest tree native to the Amazon but introduced to Asia via seed despatched from London's Royal Botanic Gardens in Kew. Rubber trees were first planted in Malaya in 1877 and a plantation was operational by 1898. The plant flourished especially in Malaysia, which had similar growing conditions to Brazil, and Malaysia became the world's leading rubber-producing nation. Rubber is made from the latex extracted from the tree, and this is done manually by carefully scoring the bark and allowing the latex to drip into a small cup. Each cup is collected some five hours later and the process continues.

Latex collection and maintaining the rubber-tree plantations is a manual process, the original workers having come mostly from South India at the turn of the twentieth century. Due to the introduction of synthetic rubber and

Latex collection in a rubber estate

fluctuating natural rubber prices, few Indians still work in the rubber estates and most now work in other professions (other Indians came to Malaysia to work in the army, as traders and as professionals).

Traders and Shopkeepers

There are numerous shops in Langkawi, especially in Kuah and the Pantai Cenang to Pantai Tengah strip. The Chinese generally concentrate in Kuah, with many still being merchants, shopkeepers and tradespeople.

Global Sailors

With four marinas catering to yachts and powerboats, there is a small and usually transient community of expatriate sailors who stop over in Langkawi on their global explorations. Langkawi is an important port for sailors moving between the Pacific and Indian Oceans via the Straits of Malacca. The facilities for servicing and repairing yachts are well developed, and are one of the reasons why some sailors stay longer in Langkawi.

There are four marinas – Royal Langkawi Yacht Club, Telaga Harbour Park and Resorts World on the main island, and Rebak Marina just offshore on Rebak Island. Repairs are possible at Rebak Marina and the Wave Master facility. Sailors can moor at a marina as well as at sheltered anchorages around the islands. These have several aspects, making Langkawi an all-season yachting destination.

Popular anchorages include Bass Harbour (near Kuah), around Pulau Timun, Pulau Bumbon, Pulau Dayang Bunting (including 'The Fjord'), Pulau Tuba, off Pantai Kok, and 'The Hole in the Wall' (south of Pulau Langgun).

Biodiversity

Langkawi ranks among the 12 mega-biologically diverse countries in the world. Because of its unique UNESCO Geopark status (p. 94), the Malaysian government has invested a considerable amount of money into developing the ecotourism sector at the Geopark. As a result, conservation efforts including community involvement, education and socio-economic factors have been paramount for developing the Geopark concept, in order to obtain a sustainable approach to tourism and the overall biodiversity of the island.

There are four main geodiversity and biodiversity areas: Machinchang Cambrian Geoforest Park, Kilim Karst Geoforest Park, Dayang Bunting Marble Geoforest Park and the Kubang Badak BioGeo Trail. Each is well known for its high biodiversity of flora and fauna, much of it considered endemic or rare, and tending to attract numerous specialized visitors to the island.

The uniqueness of the Geopark lies in the way a mangrove ecosystem can easily thrive on a limestone foundation. Island karst landscapes occur in vertical and sub-rounded karstic hills, and also in pinnacles of various shapes and sizes,

Explore the Kilim River

Visit Langkawi's wetlands by boat

separated by narrow gorges and valleys that are dominated by mangrove forests. When observing the many grey limestone karst walls, visitors are amazed by the hanging gardens of flora that are scattered with wall-clinging plants and trees, some even dating back to prehistoric times. Fossils in limestone rocks are no stranger to the naked eye, though you have to be observant to notice these prehistoric remnants.

In order to maintain this important status, various educational and awareness programmes have been enhanced by the Geopark School and Geopark Community Programme. Several Geopark Clubs have also been established at the local schools in Langkawi as a medium for disseminating information. Their approach combines economic efficiency with ecological sustainability. Tourism-industry participants around the island are briefed on a yearly basis on important updates regarding biodiversity and ecotourism changes. This is part of the measures that the Langkawi Development Authority (LADA) has been engaged in since obtaining Geopark status. LADA is widely known as the main trusted body responsible for developing Langkawi Geopark, and was appointed as a coordinator of the Geopark by the Government of Kedah in May 2006. The following year, LADA received funding from the Malaysian Ministry of Finance for the development of the Geopark.

Limestone karst topography

Geo-heritage conservation is described as a management or process that involves any effort, such as preservation, restoration, reconstruction or rehabilitation, which is suitable and focused on protecting natural assets known as geology in order to maintain the value, history and sense of place for future benefits. Ecotourism development was introduced as part of the development of the tourism concept, aiming to minimize the impact on the natural environment, and serving public education on the awareness of natural preservation. Geo-heritage conservation covers three main areas: heritage conservation, economic development and community involvement. It is one of the main objectives of the development strategy for the Langkawi Geopark area.

To date, the island has seen a considerable increase in ecotourist visitors – in 2018, there were 3.63 million visitors arriving by both air and sea. This includes visits by cruise ships that dock at the Resorts World Langkawi cruise jetty, where cruisers take up the many nature and ecotourism activities offered as day trips.

Langkawi has always been promoted as a duty-free island getaway that offers visitors beautiful beaches and luxurious resorts. On top of that, they can enjoy many tourism sub-genres, like adventure, nature, wildlife, ecotourism, culture, food, and interesting legends and folklore.

Did You Know?
OBIT is the official Langkawi UNESCO Global GeoPark mascot.
• He is named after the trilobite, one of the earliest and longest living marine animals, which flourished across vast oceans for nearly 300 million years.
• His kind thrived at the dawn of the Palaeozoic Era (often referred to as the Trilobite Age), which goes back to more than 540 million years ago.
• His top part is a carapace or hard crustacean upper shell, while the lower part is divided longitudinally into three lobes (hence 'tri' and 'lobite').
• Obit represents the oldest fossil in Malaysia, the Saukiid trilobite, which can be found within the Machinchang sandstone.

PART 2: AROUND THE ISLAND

Langkawi is one of Malaysia's largest islands and is surrounded by 98 smaller islands. Both the main island and the archipelago are named Langkawi. Unlike many other resort islands in the region, much of Langkawi is still covered in forests, and its ancient rock formations are recognized as a Geopark by UNESCO. Its flora and fauna are important and are accessible to adventurous travellers who enjoy an encounter with nature. While

While rarely crowded, Pantai Cenang is Langkawi's most popular beach

many parts are still undeveloped and only four of the islands are settled, Langkawi still offers indulgent luxuries such as deluxe resorts, restaurants for all budgets, soothing spas, marinas and duty-free shopping. With just 70,000 residents there is never a sense of being crowded out, and visitors can always find a remote and near-deserted beach should they want to truly escape.

SOUTH-WEST

After Kuah, the south-west of the island, including the two main beach precincts of Pantai Cenang and Pantai Tengah, is the most populated part of Langkawi's main island. Visitors arriving by plane touch down at Langkawi International Airport, and many stay nearby in a range of accommodation options. This is the liveliest part of the island, with shops, restaurants, bars and cafés catering to visitors.

Relax along the long, wide Pantai Tengah beach

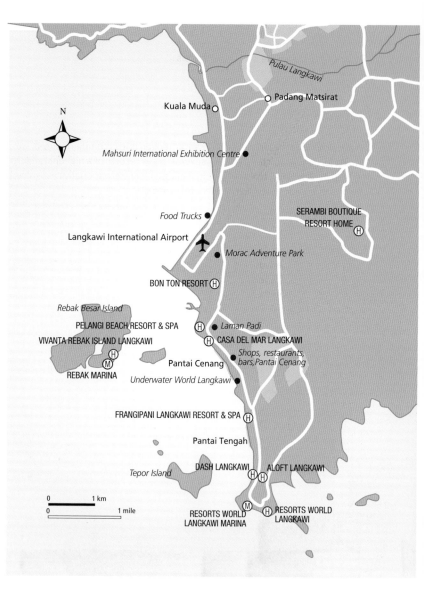

N

Pulau Langkawi

Kuala Muda ○   ○ Padang Matsirat

Mahsuri International Exhibition Centre ●

Food Trucks ●

SERAMBI BOUTIQUE
RESORT HOME Ⓗ

Langkawi International Airport ✈

● Morac Adventure Park

BON TON RESORT Ⓗ

Rebak Besar Island

PELANGI BEACH RESORT & SPA Ⓗ ● Laman Padi

VIVANTA REBAK ISLAND LANGKAWI   Ⓗ CASA DEL MAR LANGKAWI

Ⓗ
Ⓜ   ● Shops, restaurants,
REBAK MARINA   Pantai Cenang   bars, Pantai Cenang

Underwater World Langkawi ●

FRANGIPANI LANGKAWI RESORT & SPA Ⓗ

Pantai Tengah

DASH LANGKAWI   ALOFT LANGKAWI
Tepor Island   Ⓗ Ⓗ

Ⓜ Ⓗ RESORTS WORLD
RESORTS WORLD   LANGKAWI
LANGKAWI MARINA

0   1 km

0   1 mile

The southwestern part of the island, arbitrarily from just north of the airport and Padang Matsirat all the way southwards to Resorts World Langkawi and the Awana Pier, is the most developed part of the island after Kuah. It also has the most developed tourism infrastructure, such as the airport, Mahsuri International Exhibition Centre (adjoining the airport), the Pantai Cenang (pronounced 'ch nung' and occasionally spelt 'Chenang') to Pantai Tengah beachfront strip, the cruise-liner facility at Resorts World and some visitor attractions.

The 2km (1.2 mile)-stretch of Pantai Cenang is the island's most popular beach, with a rocky headland at Underwater World separating it from Pantai Tengah in the south, the second most popular beach. A one-way road (heading south) has eased congestion along the usually busy Pantai Cenang retail and entertainment precinct. Shops, restaurants, cafés and budget hotels line the beach and the other side of the road. The building density is such that over recent years there has been virtually no evidence of the beachfront and there are very few natural attractions among the commercial maze and jumble. Pantai Tengah is less commercialized, with several larger resorts of a higher standard, including a few internationally recognized hotel brands.

First staged in 1991, the Langkawi International Maritime and Aerospace exhibition (LIMA) happens every two years (odd-numbered years). It particularly attracts global defence buyers and sellers to the Mahsuri International Convention Centre adjoining the airport (the maritime exhibition is centred on Resorts World Langkawi).

Aerial view of the marina at Resorts World Langkawi

Places to Visit

Pantai Cenang

Also known as Cenang Beach, this is the best known Langkawi beach. It is wide and flat, with shallow waters that have a gentle swell and low waves, making it safe for swimming. The beach attracts tourists mostly staying in the budget accommodation immediately lining the beach or on the other side of Jalan Kuala Muda, the main road that passes through Pantai Cenang parallel to the beach.

The beach starts in the north at the Pelangi Beach Resort and Spa, and extends southwards to a rocky headland where Underwater World Langkawi is located. A variety of watersports is available, including jet skiing and parasailing. While vendors sell drinks and snacks, Cenang is recognized as a beach where people can relax without being bothered by persistent vendors walking along the beach.

Just back from the beach the main road is lined with dining outlets, bars, souvenir shops and conveniences stores, and it is especially popular as the sun goes down and the crowds relocate from the beach. There are few large shops here, the biggest shopping outlet being the two-storey Cenang Mall, with boutiques, pharmacy, fast-food and coffee concepts, duty-free shops and ATM machines.

Pantai Tengah

This is the island's second most popular beach, just to the south of Pantai Cenang. It starts in the north just beyond a headland and Underwater World, and extends southwards for about 1.8km (1.1 miles) to Dash Resort Langkawi. While the beach is public, several resorts have immediate beachfront access. Another rocky headland separates Pantai Tengah to the far southeastern tip of the island and Resorts World Langkawi.

Jalan Teluk Baru is the main road from north to south. It is mostly lined with shops, restaurants, cafés and spas, though not in the same density as at Pantai Cenang, and they dwindle just beyond Dash Resort Langkawi.

Small and mostly budget resorts line Pantai Cenang

Atma Alam Batik Art Village

Visitors can buy local Malaysian art or make their own *batik* design on silk or cotton at Langkawi's original art village, Atma Alam. There is also a *songket* gallery (*songket* is hand-woven cotton or silk intricately patterned with gold or silver thread). The gallery is located just to the east of Padang Matsirat and is open daily from 9.00 a.m. to 6.00 p.m., with free admission.

Padang Matsirat

Located just north of the airport, Padang Matsirat is the second largest township on Langkawi. Here there are shops, markets and some excellent lunchtime food stalls selling an enticing array of *nasi campur* (mixed rice). The Sunday night market offers great opportunities for locals to buy fresh produce and tasty snacks. This is also a good chance for visitors to join in the lively market action and mix with locals. The official hours are 5.30 p.m. to 10.00 p.m., but in reality many stallholders open earlier.

Laman Padi (Rice Garden Museum)

This museum at Pantai Cenang has reasonable displays and information on the importance of growing rice in *padi* (paddy) fields in Langkawi and elsewhere in Malaysia. There is a Heritage Gallery, Padi Gallery Herb Garden and Garden of Variety. Visitors have to make their own way around the displays to learn about the importance of rice and the rice-growing cycle. Kedah is known to many as Malaysia's rice bowl. Depending on the time of the year, the rice will have just been planted, or will be growing or being harvested. Scarecrows are used to frighten away some birds, although not all. The *padi* fields on the island are good for spotting egrets, herons and even the occasional raptor.

Entry to Laman Padi is free – which is good because the displays are not in peak condition. There are toilets and a small restaurant; with some luck, a member of staff can be mustered to guide you around. The entrance is opposite the Pelangi Resort, and opening hours are 9.00 a.m. to 5.00 p.m.

Those who are truly interested in rice growing can always stop at any field around the island and take a look, or consult farmers should they be in the field tending their crop.

Learn about the crop at the Rice Garden Museum

Get close to marine life at Underwater World

Underwater World Langkawi

Underwater World Langkawi, located on Pantai Cenang, is one of Asia's largest aquariums. It houses more than 5,000 marine and freshwater organisms, including turtles, sharks, rays, fish, eels and penguins. While there are some 100 tanks of varying sizes, one of the highlights involves walking through a glassed-in tunnel where you can view many species at close range, including predatory sharks, large marine turtles and rays. Visitors can also see otters, starfish, crabs, sea cucumbers and numerous colourful fish, including koi.

There is a touch pool enabling young children to engage with the marine world. There are also displays of Subantarctic Rockhopper Penguins and Black-footed Penguins. Some of the animals have specific feeding times when there is enhanced activity – for example Harbour Seals at 11.00 a.m. and 3.00 p.m. daily. The facilities are extensive, with a selection of duty-free products at the adjoining Zon Duty Free outlet, restaurants and cafés. The facility is open daily from 10.00 a.m. to 6.00 p.m., and 9.30 a.m. to 6.30 p.m. on public holidays.

Food Trucks North of the Airport

The main road north skirts the airport perimeter, and food trucks and stalls line the northern side of the runway fencing. The area is very popular with locals, who come here to buy and eat snacks beneath shady trees with gentle sea breezes flowing in from the bay. An added bonus is watching the planes arriving at or departing from the airport at close quarters.

Visitors are always welcome to pull up a plastic chair at a makeshift outlet beneath the trees to enjoy *laksa, nasi ayam,* burgers, seafood and a cool, local speciality called *air batu campur* or *ais kacang* (known as 'ABC', or shaved ice with syrup, corn, beans and condensed milk). Fishing boats moored just offshore provide the opportunity for an impressive photograph in the afternoon light.

Sunset Strip

Sunsets are another feature of Langkawi, especially along the south-east, with the beaches here having an uninterrupted view to the west. Several bars along the Pantai Cenang-Pantai Tengah strip make the most of their beachfront position.

Fishing Villages

There are several fishing communities along the coast in this part of Langkawi. It is possible to walk around villages such as Kuala Muda and Kuala Teriang, and observe a fishing fleet moored in the protective waters of streams that flow into the sea. Fishing boats are often moored along the riverbanks, and members of the fishing communities can be seen repairing their boats and other equipment. The mangrove-lined riverbanks here are also good habitats for watching wading birds.

Sports Facilities

There is a small marina in front of the Resorts World Langkawi property (previously Awana Porto Malai) at the far southeastern tip of the main island. This adjoins a pier where cruise ships occasionally berth. The boardwalk fronting the marina takes on a Mediterranean setting and includes a hotel, restaurant and some shops. Canoeing, kayaking and fishing are possible in the offshore waters of the resort. Several island-hopping operators and sunset cruise yachts use the marina as their departure point. Some yachts berth here, but the other three marinas on the island are more popular for this purpose. There are several fixed moorings offshore that some vessels use.

It is possible to join an extended jet-ski tour departing from Pantai Cenang, lasting over several hours and visiting several islands in the archipelago. Tours of four-hour duration are available, with one catering to participants from as young as three years of age. The more advanced trip takes in Pulau Dayang Bunting.

Sunset cruises typically depart at about 5.00 p.m. and return by 8.00 p.m., with a free flow of beverages and snacks (maybe a seafood barbecue) a highlight for most cruises. Some have a 'saltwater jacuzzi' suspended at the side for guests to cling on to and be gently massaged as the vessel slips through the waters of the Andaman Sea. Operators such as Crystal Yacht and Tropical Charters operate from the marina here, and head down to a few islands to the south and back. Sunset

Fishing boats moored amongst mangroves

Parasailing

conducted by operators such as Dev's Adventure Tours may also take in a rubber estate, fishing village and local market.

Skydive Langkawi is the latest aerial adventure offered on the island. For the ultimate adrenalin rush, you can join a tandem skydive and jump from 4,267m (14,000ft) with an experienced and qualified skydiving instructor, reaching a terminal velocity of 220km/h (137mph) over the island and landing on a soft sandy beach. Jumps are only made when the weather conditions are favourable. Skydive Langkawi operates strictly according to Australian Parachuting Safety Standards.

Go-kart enthusiasts can enjoy a few laps on the circuit at Morac Adventure Park near the southern side of the airport runway. The park offers a good experience for first-timers to endurance racing and simulated GP sprint racing on a fully renovated track. An onsite restaurant fuels hungry participants with various culinary styles.

Bay near Pulau Beras Besah is the place for the best photographs of the sunset. Crystal Yacht is typical in offering a dinner barbecue cruise with a free flow of chilled beverages. In addition, it operates Geopark day cruises plus private charters for groups of up to 30. Sunset cruises also depart from other locations on the island, including the Royal Langkawi Yacht Club.

Cycling is a pleasant activity in the rural back lanes, through *padi* fields just to the east of Pantai Cenang. The cycling is on flat land and is not difficult apart from the issues of the heat and humidity, although tours are mostly conducted in the cool of the day. Excursions of 3–4 hours duration (total distance of about 25km/16 miles)

Island-hopping boat

Places to Stay

There is more accommodation in this part of Langkawi than anywhere else on the island, with a great range of options, from boutique properties to beachside resorts (including the ParkRoyal, to open soon on Pantai Tengah). Most are locally operated, with Pelangi Beach Resort and Spa being one of the largest and best established. This 355-room property covers 14ha (35 acres) with a 1km (0.6 mile)-beachfront, making it one of Langkawi's best-located properties. Guests stay in wooden chalets with private balconies, and relax on the beach or by one of two pools.

Casa Del Mar is a 34-room property at the northern end of Pantai Cenang. It offers rooms from seaview to beachfront studio suites, and individualized service. Due to its relatively small size, visitors with children may want to choose a bigger resort. Guests enjoy beachfront dining at La Luna and cool drinks around La Sal's Pool Bar. There is a spa and numerous watersports activities.

The 208-room Aloft Langkawi Pantai Tengah is one of the few internationally branded hotels in the south-east. Like some hotels, it does not have immediate beach frontage, but the golden sands are just a few minutes' walk away.

Dash Resort Langkawi on Pantai Tengah has a hip atmosphere with a colonial ambiance. Dash Beach Club is a lively bar with music where the young and adventurous love to party.

Larger, budget hotels include Holiday Villa, Favehotel, Federal Villa Beach Resort, Aseania Resort and Spa, Century Langkasuka Resort and Langkawi Lagoon Sea Village.

There are numerous homestays and local budget hotels. Some smaller, more personalized choices in the south-east include Sunset Beach Resort, Ambong Ambong Langkawi Rainforest Retreat, Temple Tree and Smith House (in Padang Matsirat).

Two green hotels in the south-east are Bon Ton Resort and Frangipani Langkawi Resort and Spa (p. 144).

Picturesque pool at Pelangi Beach Resort

NORTH-WEST

Langkawi's north-west is dominated by the towering peak of Gunung Machinchang at 713m (2,339ft). Several deluxe and luxury resorts have sea views and forested backdrops along parts of the coast. Much of the area remains forested, and there are trails into the rainforest interior, waterfalls and mangroves in some coastal areas.

Aerial view of Burau Bay and Burau Island

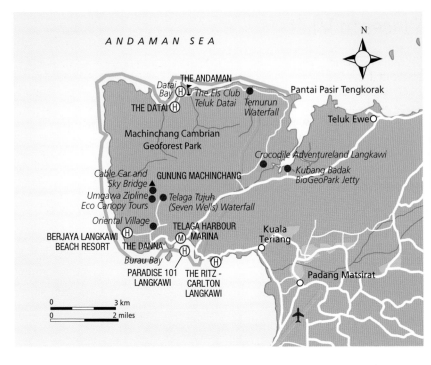

The forested slopes of Gunung Machinchang dominate the northwestern parts of the main island. A skycab (cable car) slowly ascends the traverse to the summit, and the island views and those into southern Thailand make it well worth the journey.

There are several activities close to Oriental Village, the base station for the cable car. The walk to Telaga Tujuh is probably the most walked nature trail on Langkawi. It is steep, and passes through rainforest and ends up at the base of an impressive waterfall. Seven spring-fed pools provide refreshing places to swim in cool mountain streams.

Adventurous visitors can go horse riding or ziplining through the rainforest in this part of Langkawi. Some sailors choose to moor their yachts in Telaga Harbour, while other visitors call at the bars and restaurants of the surrounding Perdana Quay. There are several accommodation options along the southern coastline of the north-west.

Gunung Machinchang separates Burau Bay from Teluk Datai, but a road around the mountain's base eventually reaches Teluk Datai, which is a dead end. The road is a pleasant drive with most traffic heading to the two luxury resorts (the Andaman site is being redeveloped after a fire) at the end of the road or the highly regarded Els Club Teluk Datai golf course. Visitor attractions along the road include, a waterfall and a few near-deserted beaches with views over the neighbouring islands of southern Thailand.

Places to Visit

Telaga Harbour and Perdana Quay

Luxury yachts moor in Telaga Harbour, which was created after extensive earthworks excavated a substantive area of coastal land. Malaysian Customs and Immigration receive and process visitors arriving from Thailand (Tarutao Marine National Park) in the marina. Those arriving by yacht from the west are guided into the marina via a stately lighthouse. All foreign yachts have to notify the Harbour Master and be processed by the Malaysian Customs and Immigration located here.

The marina, with its surrounding Perdana Quay and backdrop of Gunung Machinchang, is picturesque. Several restaurants, bars and cafés line Perdana Quay – the best time to visit is to dine alfresco along the boardwalk alongside the marina. A petrol station and ATM machine are located on the eastern side of the marina. The Danna is an impressive colonial-style luxury hotel within walking distance of the marina precinct.

Langkawi Skycab and Oriental Village

An exhilarating skycab gondola ride can be taken across the forest canopy and up the escarpment to Gunung Machinchang's summit at 713m (2,339ft). The 2km

Telaga Harbour at the base of Mount Machinchang

(1.2 mile)-journey, opened in 2002, is one of the world's steepest (42° incline), with a rise of 680m (2,231ft); views over the island and into southern Thailand are superb. There are two stops along the way – Middle Station (650m/2,133ft) and Top Station (708m/2,333ft). There are viewing platforms, interpretative signs and refreshment outlets at both.

On the journey to and from the summit, visitors can observe the ancient rocky outcrops in Machinchang Cambrian Geoforest Park, the rainforest and mountain flora, plus the birdlife. The topography varies, with cliffs, deep chasms, rock chimneys, pinnacles and overhangs being just some of the features. There are several walks between the stations to enable a closer look at the rocks and the lowland dipterocarp forest vegetation.

The Langkawi Sky Bridge, opened in 2004, is a short walk from Top Station. This suspended bridge is the longest free-span and curved bridge in the world, and it provides a unique perspective over the rainforest canopy. The structure is supported by a single 82m (269ft) pylon, thus enabling visitors to have a 100m (328ft) high view over the forested landscape. Associated activities here include a 6D Cinemotion, SkyDome, SkyRex, 3D Art Museum, SkyBoutique, Galeri Produk Langkawi, Imaginarium, F1 Simulator, One Stop Centre and SkyAdventure Park.

Oriental Village expands around a constructed lake at the base terminus. This shopping, dining and budget hotel precinct is a popular place to stroll around before or after experiencing the cable car. Oriental Village is open daily from 10.00 a.m. to 10.00 p.m.

The cable car located at Burau Bay has variable opening hours, but is mostly open from 9.30 a.m. to 7.00 p.m. (slightly longer hours for the Langkawi weekend) depending on the weather, with the service being suspended during periods of high winds. There is a chargeable express lane for those in a hurry.

Telaga Tujuh (Seven Wells)

This beautiful series of seven cascades and pools is located deep within the forested areas in the foothills of Gunung Machinchang. The main attraction is a 91m (299ft) waterfall and several spring-fed ponds at its base. The forested trail to the waterfall begins just a few kilometres beyond the Oriental Village. There is a shop in the car park where snacks and drinks can be bought – it is advisable to stay well hydrated on the walk.

The well-formed trail of some 900 steps is steep and passes through mature rainforest supporting persistent macaques (try to ignore them and do not encourage them by feeding them). Take your time, as there is plenty to see in the forest, especially at the macro level for sightings of insects, vines and detail in the rainforest understorey. Toilet and changing room facilities are located at the top of the trail.

Adventurous visitors can continue deeper into the forest to swim in cool mountain pools. Note that the granite rock surrounding the pools can be slippery so keeping well back from the edges and on the viewing platform is advised.

For those seeking an alternative rainforest experience, alight from the cable car and walk down the mountain. Bear in mind that this is best done with a knowledgeable guide.

Umgawa Zipline Eco Adventures

The adventure sport of ziplining is strategically located between the skycab and Telaga Tujuh Waterfalls, with the meeting point being just off the waterfall car park.

Umgawa Zipline involves up to 12 ziplines, three sky bridges and one thrilling abseil descent in the rainforest treetops surrounding Gunung Machinchang. Participants choose either the Big Waterfall Adventure, which lasts in excess of two hours, with the highest point being at 80m (262ft) and the longest line being 200m (656ft). The shorter Jungle Flight of about one hour covers six ziplines, one sky bridge and an abseil descent.

Two guides attend to the technical side of the activity while explaining some of the rainforest flora and fauna. One of the lines (the Honeymoon Line) is a double line that is especially aimed at couples. Umgawa Zipline is open daily from 8.30 a.m. to 4.30 p.m.

Paradise 101

This private day resort recreational island is located just off Telaga Harbour at Pantai Kok. It is an artificial island now covered with towering casuarina trees, and is home to numerous watersports, and other recreational and relaxing activities. Visitors can buy various packages covering recreation, food and beverages, and can swim or relax under shady trees, or be more active on a zipline, or by kayaking, banana-boat riding, jet skiing or parasailing. There are also an aqua park, sunset deck and music events in the evening. A shuttle service operates from Pantai Cenang, and the island's facilities are available for private events. The facility is open from 10.00 a.m. until the late hours.

Pantai Kok

This once public beach appears to now be closed to the public, with villas from the neighbouring Danna encroaching on

Join an exhilarating zipline over the rainforest canopy

to the beachfront immediately adjacent to the resort. Mutiara Burau Bay Resort once fronted both Burau Bay and Pantai Kok but has closed, and the site's redevelopment appears to have stalled. There were plans to develop the site that adjoins the Berjaya property and to extend on to the nearby island of Pulau Burau.

Gardens of Rainbows and Butterflies

Langkawi is a superb place in which to see butterflies (of some 1,000 butterfly species recorded in Malaysia, half can be found in Langkawi). There are many in a natural setting at Darulaman Sanctuary near the base of Gunung Raya. At these established gardens close to Pantai Kok and the Danna, thousands of butterflies can be seen feeding on the nectar of numerous flowering plants. There are water ponds and fountains, plus walk-in

Admire Langkawi's prolific butterflies

domes that enclose plants and butterflies for closer inspection. The butterflies are most active in the early morning and late afternoon, especially on clear days. The gardens are open daily from 9.00 a.m. to 6.00 p.m., and there is an entry fee.

Taman Buaya (Crocodile Adventureland Langkawi)

Formerly known as the Crocodile Farm, Taman Buaya houses more than 1,000 crocodiles on a large property just off the road to Teluk Datai. Elevated access enables visitors to get close to these huge reptiles in safety. The farm is open daily from 9.00 a.m. to 6.00 p.m., with an entry fee. Souvenirs, snacks and drinks are available.

Temurun Waterfall

This impressive series of waterfalls (there are three tiers), with a cumulative drop of 200m (656ft), is located just off the road to Teluk Datai in a scenic rainforest setting. Most visitors take the short walk from the car park to the final cascade into a pond at the base of the falls. Several pools here make for a refreshing change to swimming in the sea on the coastal side of the road.

Layers of sandstone and shale deposited as sedimentary rocks are slowly being eroded by the falls. Like all waterfalls, these ones are most impressive during or just after rain (especially during the rainy months of September and October), although caution needs to be exercised during heavy flows. Crab-eating Macaques frequent the picnic area and swimming ponds at the falls' base. The falls are located on the south side of the road, halfway between the Crocodile Adventureland Langkawi and Teluk Datai.

Pantai Pasir Tengkorak

This is one of the most secluded and least visited beaches in Langkawi – perfect for those who want to get away from it all. The forest comes close to the waterline, ensuring excellent shade for those who seek limited exposure to the sun. The beach overlooks the islands of neighbouring Thailand and is only visited during the Langkawi weekend, as it is popular with the locals.

Sports Facilities

The premier golf course on the island is the superb Els Club Teluk Datai, located at Teluk Datai and set in rainforest that borders the Andaman Sea. The course, designed by four-time major winner Ernie Els ('The Big Easy'), is rated by many who play it as one of the best they have encountered. The par-72, 6,172m (6,750yd) golf course was recognized as the best in Asia when it reopened in 2014 after Els renovated the original course

Explore rainforests in many ways

that first opened in 1992. Five of the most picturesque holes face the water and there are no bunkers. The layout was determined by fairway alignments

Swim at the near-deserted Pasir Tengkorak beach

Award-winning Els Club Teluk Datai

between the forest, large trees and a meandering stream.

Tee off times are from 7.30 a.m. to 4.30 p.m., and buggies, equipment and shoes are available for rent. The golf course includes a fully grassed driving range, practice putt and chop greens, and a clubhouse with a cafés and lockers.

The Langkawi IRONMAN 70.3 staged in October attracts global multi-sports athletes (swimming, cycling and running) to this part of Langkawi. Some 2,500 athletes start this gruelling race in the waters off Pantai Kok. The top 40 in the Langkawi race gain a place to compete in the IRONMAN 70.3 World Championship. The Langkawi race is part of 235 multi-sports events contested in 55 countries.

Island Horses operates from near Oriental Village for riders of all abilities. Novice riders may take a first-time ride on a lead rope, while experienced riders can head off into the secondary rainforest for an extended ride along jungle trails. Most riders have the opportunity to experience riding along rainforest trails, as well as to canter along the sands of Pantai Kok. Staff select a horse to match a rider's ability. The facility is open every day from 8.30 a.m. to 12.30 p.m. and 2.00 p.m. to 5.30 p.m., except on Monday. Most rides begin at 9.00 a.m. or 4.00 p.m., and most are of one- or two-hour duration. Every Saturday at 5.00 p.m., the staff stage a horse show at the Perdana Stables in Langkawi.

Skytrex Adventure Langkawi, located in the forest of Burau Bay at Perdana Quay, offers a thrilling way to experience the coastal rainforest. There are three challenging adventure courses through the forest – Little Legend (beginners), Eagle Thrill (intermediate) and Island Extreme (advanced). Participants explore the rainforest canopy by climbing, walking, crawling, gliding and using high-rope courses. They can also admire the dramatic landscape of Gunung Machinchang. The park is open daily from 9.00 a.m. to 5.00 p.m.

Places to Stay

Berjaya Langkawi Resort has a commanding position at the base of Gunung Machinchang, along the coastline of Burau Bay and 8km (5 miles) from the airport. It has a southerly aspect with villas extending over the water and up into the rainforest. It is an expansive resort, and a fleet of buggies transfers guests to and from their rooms. Guests have access to Teluk Burau (Burau Bay), one of the most picturesque beaches on the island. Some of the finest rooms are the premium seaview chalets with uninterrupted views across the Andaman Sea. Guests can relax within the rainforest in Taaras Spa and dine in an over-the-water Thai restaurant, Chinese restaurant, or beachside brasserie, or sip cool beverages in a beachside bar. In addition to the inevitable macaques, this is also a good location to see the Dusky Leaf Monkey.

The Danna Langkawi is located along the nearby beachfront within Telaga Harbour Park. What was once public beach access along parts of Pantai Kok now appears to be the exclusive domain of the resort, comprising 135 rooms and 10 luxurious beachfront villas. It has grand colonial-style architecture with an expansive iron *porte cochère*. The rooms and pool are large, and all the villas have their own private infinity pools. Guests have direct beach access, can relax in the hotel's spa, dine in one of several outlets and are pampered by personalized service.

The 121-room The Datai has always been one of the island's most prestigious properties. Located on Teluk Datai,

adjoining the Andaman, it has been refurbished and has incorporated many green practices (p. 144).

Temporarily closed due to a fire at the premises in January 2021, The Andaman is close enough to appreciate the cool sea breezes of Teluk Datai, but is well camouflaged by a strip of coastal rainforest that was retained when it was constructed. There is coral in the bay and the resort has an activity regeneration programme to ensure that it remains in place. Under the resort's coral-conservation programme, the Andaman Reef damaged in the 2004 tsunami is being reinstated. Guests can participate in a private guided snorkel tour over the onsite coral nursery. Its Jentayu Lounge is a place for a sunset drink; it is also a great location to see Colugos in the evening.

The 119-room Ritz-Carlton Langkawi, like most other luxury properties on Langkawi, has a back-to-nature ambiance. Private villas extend into the surrounding coastal rainforest and over the waterfront.

Aerial view of Berjaya Langkawi Resort

NORTH

Langkawi's north is sparsely settled, but it includes the popular beachside holiday destination of Tanjung Rhu and vast expanses of mangrove forests that fringe much of the coastline. Parts of the Kilim Karst Geopark in the north are close to Tanjung Rhu and

Langkawi's north has several luxury resorts

extend into the northeastern and eastern parts of the main island. The Kubang Badak BioGeoPark is also located here. Tours into the mangroves are one of the most popular eco-activities in Langkawi.

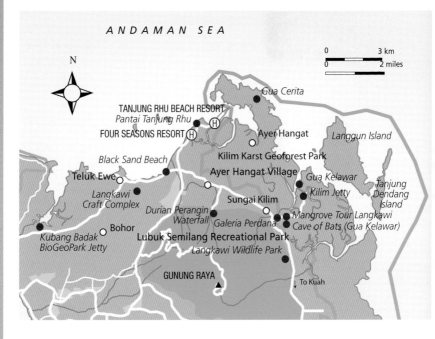

ANDAMAN SEA

N

0   3 km
0   2 miles

Gua Cerita

TANJUNG RHU BEACH RESORT
Pantai Tanjung Rhu
FOUR SEASONS RESORT
Ayer Hangat
Langgun Island

Black Sand Beach
Kilim Karst Geoforest Park
Teluk Ewe
Ayer Hangat Village
Gua Kelawar
Tanjung Dendang Island
Langkawi Craft Complex
Kilim Jetty
Durian Perangin Waterfall
Sungai Kilim
Bohor
Galeria Perdana
Mangrove Tour Langkawi
Kubang Badak BioGeoPark Jetty
Lubuk Semilang Recreational Park
Cave of Bats (Gua Kelawar)
Langkawi Wildlife Park
GUNUNG RAYA
To Kuah

Much of the north of the main island is undeveloped, with extensive stands of mangrove forests along a maze of inlets. There are some beaches along the north, with the best being the domain of exclusive resorts such as the Four Seasons Resort Langkawi and Tanjung Rhu. Many mangrove tours depart from the north from the jetty near Tanjung Rhu, the recreational beachfront south-west of the Four Seasons, the Kilim Geopark Jetty and the most recent departure point at Kubang Badak BioGeoPark Jetty.

Extensive outcrops of limestone can be found in the north, with a large quarry located at Teluk Ewe. Here, a substantial jetty is used to ship the cement from the integrated cement works to other parts of the country, where it is used in the construction industry. The fishing community that lives here uses a smaller, older wooden jetty to the east, along Pantai Pasir Hitam (Black Sand Beach).

Places to Visit

Gua Cerita (Cave of Legends)
This cave on Langkawi's north coast is accessible by boat only, and is often visited on mangrove tour boats travelling from Tanjung Rhu to Sungai Kilim Geopark. Visitors land on the beach then ascend a flight of steps. Some cave paintings add intrigue and mystery to the site.

Kubang Badak BioGeoPark
Kubang Badak BioGeoPark, Langkawi's most recent Geopark site, extends beyond the jetty just off Jalan Teluk Yu, one of

Mangroves protect the coastline

species. Offshore islands like this are important as they protect the foreshore from soil erosion, strong winds and waves rolling in from the open Andaman Sea. They are also key spawning grounds for fish and crustaceans. Members of the fishing community can be seen rowing traditional wooden boats out to their fishing boats or to fishing traps just offshore.

the main roads that cross the north of the island. The village of Kampung Kubang Badak is located on this road and is a part of Langkawi where Thai is spoken and understood by many. Not surprisingly, its original settlers came from neighbouring then Siam (now Thailand) decades ago. The maritime border with Thailand is just a few kilometres offshore, and those using a Malaysian mobile phone provider may find that as they venture offshore from the jetty, their phones switch to a Thai network.

While some of the locals still fish the waters here for mullet, prawns and mantis shrimp, many now work in service industries such as tourism. Mangrove tours operate from the jetty, out into the protected inlet and past the mangrove-covered island of Pulau Kubang Badak. Visitors can often see playful Smooth-coated Otters (p. 103) in the water, especially after the fishing boats return from sea.

The variation between high and low tides here is pronounced, and the offshore island of Pulau Kubang Badak comprises silt and mud that is deposited by the changing tide. Over time, the accumulated layers of deposits have become colonized by mangroves, which are pioneering plant

Kompleks Kraf (Craft and Cultural Complex)

This expansive complex houses displays of pewter, *batik*, textiles, beads, jewellery, baskets and local art. Some of these are produced by local artisans who operate and demonstrate from here, while others are merely retail outlets selling handicrafts sourced from around the region. The facilities here include two museums – the Custom and Wedding Museum and the Heritage Museum – which offer an insight into Malaysian culture. There is also a restaurant and toilets, and entry is free. The centre is open from 10.00 a.m. to 6.00 p.m.

See handicrafts being made by artisans and buy their handiwork at the Craft and Cultural Complex

Pantai Pasir Hitam (Black Sand Beach)

Dark minerals such as tourmaline and ilmenite, which have eroded from nearby granite outcrops, have discoloured the sand along the beach located between Teluk Ewe and Kampung Padang Lalang at the turn-off north for Tanjung Rhu. Despite efforts by the authority to turn this into a tourist attraction, the mostly silica sand with some black minerals is not black, nor is it a place justifying a specific journey. The old wooden jetty and fishing fleet may be more interesting to many than the flecks of black minerals. There is ample parking and some facilities, including shops selling souvenirs and snacks.

Tanjung Rhu

The glistening, fine white sands of Tanjung Rhu Beach are rated the best in Langkawi. They are also the hottest so use of footwear is highly recommended. The secluded beach is shallow and wide, with the only shade provided at the rear of the beach beneath towering casuarina trees.

Tanjung Rhu's white sands

While the Tanjung Rhu Resort occupies the best position, visitors can walk from the northern end along the beach and swim in the shallow waters. Super-low tides in March enable the resort's guests to walk through shallow water almost to Chabang Island. At other times, many walk out into the shallows for a considerable distance.

The road to the Tanjung Rhu Resort, just after the turn-off at the roundabout in Padang Lalang Village, passes a stretch of public beach. There are a few restaurants, including a famous fish and chip outlet on the beach, and makeshift booking offices for mangrove tours and watersports just off the beach.

Durian Perangin Waterfall

This small waterfall situated 2km (1.3 miles) south from the main road between Air Hangat Village and Galeria Perdana is a pleasant retreat, where only a few tourists venture. It is popular during weekends with the locals, who come here to picnic in a few shelters and to bathe in the cool stream water. The 14-tier waterfall is accessible via a short trail through the rainforest.

Enjoy a waterfall picnic

Ayer Hangat Village

Local legend and geology have different explanations for the origins of the hot springs found in several pools here. Mineral-rich water in some of the pools ranges from 38° C to 42° C, providing therapeutic qualities that include soothing relief for those with aching joints. Private jacuzzis fed by natural hot spring water are available for hire. Facilities include toilets, showers, food stalls and numerous other stalls selling souvenirs. The saltwater hot springs in the village are one of just eight such facilities in the world.

Kilim Karst Geoforest Park and Mangrove Tours

One of the most popular departure points for mangrove tours is Kilim Jetty just to the north off the main road (Jalan Ayer Hangat) near Galeria Perdana. Visitors have the opportunity to see the fascinating mangroves with their aerial roots, and to learn about how they assist in protecting the coast from storm and even tsunami damage. Mudflats are where crabs, lizards and waterbirds can be seen. The steep limestone cliffs that fringe the mangroves are equally impressive. Various

A kayak gets you close to mangroves

geological formations can be seen, with limestone caves being the most obvious. Most mangrove tours stop at caves such as Gua Kelawar (Bat Cave), or pass through at low tide, for example at Gua Buaya (Crocodile Cave).

One of the big attractions are the raptors, such as the Brahminy Kite and White-breasted Sea Eagle, soaring on thermals above or close to the water as they hunt for fish. Choose your tour operator carefully to ensure that they do not feed any animal matter to the birds along the way. Unscrupulous operators throw chicken gut into the water to attract the raptors, and while this may be good for those seeking close-up photos, the practice is ecologically unsound as these birds do not normally feed on chicken and it disrupts their feeding cycle.

The Hole in the Wall Fish Farm is often visited on mangrove tours departing from here. The fish are retained in large nets until they develop fully before being

Brahminy Kite soaring over wetlands

harvested. Visitors can learn about how they are raised, as well as see many different types of marine organism that are housed here, including stingrays.

Some companies, such as Dev's Adventure, offer kayak tours among the mangroves to enable a good look at this significant ecosystem and the fauna that thrives here. Exploring the mangrove forest by kayak allows you to discover smaller channels and get very close to the aerial roots of the mangroves, while exercising. The day normally starts early, before the waters become disturbed by other boats and before the full heat of the day. The overhanging mangrove branches provide good shade in the narrowest of channels.

Visitors should allocate half a day, including hotel transfer, for a mangrove tour. While most tours cater to mainstream tourism, there are specialist nature guides who share their insightful knowledges and can take keen birdwatchers to isolated parts of the mangroves away from the most visited areas.

Galeria Perdana

This gallery houses the various awards, souvenirs and gifts given to the former Malaysian Prime Minister, Tun Dr Mahathir Mohamad, and his wife during the various tenures of his leadership. It

is open daily from 8.30 a.m. to 5.30 p.m., with an admission charge.

Galeria Perdana

Taman Hidupan Liar (Langkawi Wildlife Park)

This attraction covering 2.2ha (5.5 acres) originally opened in 2002 as Langkawi Bird Paradise. It enables visitors to have close interaction with some 150 species and more than 2,500 local and exotic birds and other animals housed in the tropical gardens. Most are birds from Malaysia, Asia, Africa, South America and Australia. They include macaws, cockatoos, flamingos, ducks, pheasants, parrots and raptors. Some birds are housed in a walk-in aviary. Reptiles such as snakes, crocodiles and lizards are also on display.

There are fully covered walkways between displays to make this an attraction that can be visited even when the monsoon rains fall. Children have the opportunity to get close to many animals

Mangroves

A meaningful quote from a humble fisherman from Trang Province, southern Thailand:

'If there are no mangrove forests, then the sea will have no meaning. It is like having a tree with no roots, for the mangroves are the roots of the sea.'

and even feed them. There are specific feeding times for some animals, and these are the best times to see them. Onsite facilities include a souvenir shop, duty-free outlet, cafeteria and photographic area. The park is open daily from 8.30 a.m. to 6.00 p.m., although the attraction officially closes at 7.30 p.m.

Places to Stay

There are few international resorts in the immediate north of the island, but the two that exist are rated among the island's best.

The Four Seasons at Tanjung Rhu is a 16ha (39.6 acre)-hideaway along a 1.5km (1 mile)-stretch of beachfront. This luxurious 91-room property combines Moorish and local architectural styles that are noticeable in all public areas, beachside pavilions and villas secluded among coastal landscaping. The serene, secluded location appeals to those who

enjoy relaxing over leisurely dinners, soothing treatments in the Geo Spa, yoga classes, sunrise guided nature walks and cooking classes. The accommodation ranges from garden-located villas of minimum size 68m^2 (732ft^2), up to a five-bedroom Imperial Villa of 4,810m^2 (51,774ft^2) with two private pools. The Rumah Ikan Fish House offers guests the opportunity to learn about traditional methods of catching fish from the adjoining Andaman Sea. A member of the local fishing community fishes here and passes on his knowledge to guests, who can also join in the activity.

Tanjung Rhu Resort is considered one of the most private and peaceful resorts in Langkawi. Located at the end of Tanjung Rhu, the resort has three unique swimming pools – an adults-only pool, a saltwater sand pool and a sunset pool. It has its own in-house craft centre, while Mandara Spa offers an extensive menu of pampering treatments.

Get close to animals at Langkawi Wildlife Park

EAST and SOUTH-EAST

Kuah, at the far south-east of the main island, is the most populous part of Langkawi. Offices, government departments, duty-free shops, accommodation ranging from budget to luxury, restaurants and the ferry terminal to the mainland are located here. Immediately north of Kuah, the southeastern part of the island is mostly forested on the western and eastern sides of the rural road heading north.

Ferries to the mainland and southern Thailand provide a vital link for the locals and adventurous tourists

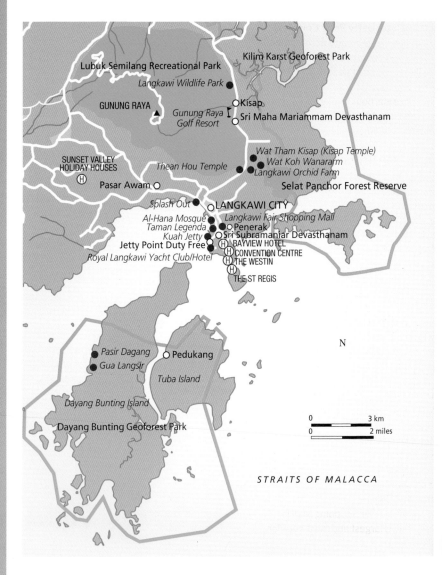

Kilim Karst Geoforest Park

Lubuk Semilang Recreational Park

Langkawi Wildlife Park

GUNUNG RAYA O **Kisap**

Gunung Raya Golf Resort O Sri Maha Mariammam Devasthanam

Wat Tham Kisap (Kisap Temple)
Wat Koh Wanararm

SUNSET VALLEY HOLIDAY HOUSES *Thean Hou Temple* *Langkawi Orchid Farm*

Selat Panchor Forest Reserve

(H) **Pasar Awam** O

Splash Out O **LANGKAWI CITY**

Al-Hana Mosque *Langkawi Fair Shopping Mall*
Taman Legenda **Penerak**
Kuah Jetty O Sri Subramaniar Devasthanam
Jetty Point Duty Free (H) **BAYVIEW HOTEL**
Royal Langkawi Yacht Club/Hotel (H) **CONVENTION CENTRE**
(H) **THE WESTIN**
(H)
THE ST REGIS

N

Pasir Dagang O **Pedukang**
Gua Langsir

Tuba Island

Dayang Bunting Island

Dayang Bunting Geoforest Park

| 0 | | 3 km |
| 0 | | 2 miles |

STRAITS OF MALACCA

Much of the eastern side of the main island is undeveloped and covered in forests like the Selat Panchor Forest Reserve. A few settlements are connected to the main centres via rural roads.

However, this is also where the main town of Kuah (often referred to as Kuah Town) is located, along with government offices, shops and services.

Visitors travelling by ferry arrive

at Kuah Jetty (Jetty Point Complex). Malaysian Customs and Immigration receive and process those arriving from Thailand (Satun) at the jetty. Those arriving by yacht from the east have to notify the Harbour Master here and be processed by Malaysian Customs and Immigration officials as well.

Duty-free Shopping and Markets

Markets are always popular with visitors, and locals particularly enjoy a night market, or *pasar malam*. Night markets are held on different nights of the week, with the Pekan Kuah market staged every Wednesday and Saturday night from 5.30 to 10.00 p.m. near the commercial heart of Kuah. Makeshift stalls are set up late in the afternoon and disassembled later. Fresh produce and snacks are especially popular, with fruits, vegetables and fish sold fresh. Snacks and drinks are on offer, and some stallholders even set up tables and chairs for their patrons.

There is a food market in Kelibang about 6km (3.7 miles) to the west of Kuah Jetty. Known as Pasar Awam Kuah, it is located just off Jalan Padang Matsirat (the main road between the airport and Kuah), and is renowned for fresh produce including fish, fruits and vegetables. It starts at about 7.00 a.m. and concludes at around 8.00 p.m.

Langkawi Fair Shopping Mall is Langkawi's largest and most popular shopping centre in the Western sense, with some 100 outlets. It contains a wide range of local and imported items such as clothes, souvenirs, handicrafts, shoes, eyewear, fashion accessories, jewellery, chocolates, perfumes, electrical appliances and cameras. Branded outlets are available in a small duty-free department store, and there are several food and beverage outlets, including fast-food concerns. A money changer and ATM services are available here. Langkawi Fair is located in Kuah, opposite Legenda Park and adjacent to the LADA building. It is five minutes from the ferry terminal and a 30-minute drive from Langkawi International Airport. Jetty Point Duty Free is located at Jetty Point. In addition to duty-free alcohol outlets, there are shops, restaurants and tourist services.

When completed, Langkawi City development, covering 11.5ha (28.5 acres), will include a 138m (453ft) spire (with observation deck at 102m/335ft above sea level), luxury hotel, marina, premium shopping outlets and upmarket residences. The development is being constructed near the waterfront to the west of Kuah.

Most shops in Kuah offer duty-free goods

Places to Visit

Rubber Estates

Extensive rubber estates are located near Kisap between Langkawi Wildlife Park in the north and Gunung Raya Golf Club in the south. The trees, which stand in neat rows, are tapped daily by workers who rise early to obtain their latex.

Initially, Langkawi's Indian population came to the island from South India to work on the rubber estates located on either side of the main road on the eastern side of the island. At one stage Malaysia was the largest natural rubber producer in the world, and it remains a dominant force. Some 90 per cent of natural rubber producers in Malaysia work as smallholders on estates covering less than 16ha (40 acres).

It has been estimated that as much as half of Malaysia's 1.07 million hectares (2.6 million acres) of rubber estates have been abandoned due to the declining global price of natural rubber. This has been exacerbated by aging trees (which

Ferry visitors arrive at Jetty Point

produce less latex) and aging workers (young people seek employment in more lucrative industries).

Kuah Jetty

Visitors arriving or departing Langkawi by ferry for the mainland (Kuala Perlis and Kuala Kedah), Penang and Thailand (Satun) use Kuah Jetty. Jetty Point is a two-storey facility that includes duty-free shops, restaurants, ATMs and services. A large car park and taxi services are located at the entrance for transfers to all parts of the island.

Visit a rubber estate to see how latex is collected

good and there is some information on Langkawi's geological past and the island's mythology. There is a jogging track, toilets, shade, and an avenue of trees that appeals to local photographers.

Splash Out Langkawi

While most tourists travel to Langkawi to enjoy its numerous beaches, others are attracted to water theme parks such as Splash Out Langkawi, located near the waterfront just west of Kuah. There are 12 slides and rides, as well as simulated waves and an expansive artificial lagoon and wave pool, plus an onsite food court and retail shop.

Dataran Lang (Eagle Square)

A 12m (39ft) high statue of a Brahminy Kite, or *helang*, is situated at the water's edge near the ferry terminal in Kuah. This bird of prey is the symbol of Langkawi. The parkland here is a popular place for strolling, taking photos and enjoying picnics.

Taman Legenda

Taman Legenda, or Legenda Park, is a pleasant coastal park immediately adjacent to Dataran Lang and just north of Kuah Jetty. While some of the facilities are not in peak condition, the views are

Langkawi Orchid Farm

This 1.2ha (3 acre)-organic farm is located about 3km (2 miles) north-east of Kuah Jetty and just to the east of Jalan Ayer Hangat near Wat Koh Wanararm. About 200 orchid species are grown here, including some rare varieties such as Tiger, Antelope and Dancing Lady Orchids. There is an entry charge with guided tours offered, and the opportunity to admire the orchids and activities such as composting and fish farming. The farm is open daily from 8.30 a.m. to 6.00 p.m

Sports Facilities

Gunung Raya Golf Resort is an 18-hole, par-72 course and driving range located on the eastern side of Gunung Raya to the north of Kuah. Facilities include a clubhouse, pro shop and buggies. The Max Wexler-designed 6,228m (6,877yd) course covers 124ha (300 acres) of former rubber estate land. Tee off times are from 7.00 a.m. to 3.30 p.m. for an 18-hole round, but as late as 5.30 p.m. for nine holes.

Malaysia's largest marina, the Royal Langkawi Yacht Club (RLYC), is located in Kuah, just a 150m (492ft) walk from Jetty Point. The protected marina can accommodate more than 250 yachts, and includes berths for large vessels like mega yachts up to 90m (295ft) long. The clubhouse here and Fisherman's Wharf cater not only to boaters using the marina, but also to visitors seeking a pleasant, relaxing venue for a drink and meal while admiring the sunset.

There are facilities here for yacht chandlery, chartering and brokering. Other services include a diving company, travel agent, boutiques, a spa and duty-free shops, in addition to bars, restaurants and cafés. Charlie's Bar and Grill is one of the best-known bars on the island. Accommodation is available in the

Enjoy marina views from the bar at Royal Langkawi Yacht Club

Langkawi Yacht Club Hotel.

The RLYC is associated with two of Asia's most prestigious yachting events. The Raja Muda Selangor International Regatta (RMSIR) is Asia's second oldest yacht race and Southeast Asia's most challenging sailing event. It is organized annually by the Royal Selangor Yacht Club (RSYC) on the outskirts of Kuala Lumpur in association with the Royal Ocean Racing Club and the Malaysia Sailing Association, assisted by the Royal Malaysia Police and Royal Malaysian Navy. The regatta was established in 1990 by, among others, the RSYC's Royal Patron, the Sultan of Selangor, HRH Sultan Sharafuddin Idris Shah (who was then the Raja Muda of Selangor).

The event is held in November, which typically marks the height of the north-east monsoon on Peninsular Malaysia, when sailors can expect conditions from glassy waters and light breezes, to a sea rolling with 2m (6.5ft) swells or higher, and 30-knot squalls blowing off the coast. The boats sail in overnight passage races along Malaysia's west coast, where they push off from the starting point in Port Klang on a course that takes them through the Straits of Malacca to checkpoints at Pangkor, Penang and Langkawi. Once in Langkawi, the boats compete in inshore harbour races. Competing yachts range from top-class IRC1 racers to classic cruisers with long overhangs dating back over 100 years. Skippers and crew have to cope with the unpredictable weather, changing tactics and heavy shipping traffic in the Straits of Malacca.

Known for its unpredictable winds, weather and tides, the RMSIR provides excitement for the most experienced sailor, along with an interesting challenge.

Sightseeing and fun social events, especially at the race's end in Langkawi, ensure the popularity of the event.

The other major yachting event is the Royal Langkawi International Regatta convened by the RLYC and contested each year in January. Local and regional yachts compete for the Prime Minister's Challenge Trophy over five days of racing.

Regattas attract international yachts

Places of Worship

There are several places of worship in this part of Langkawi, including mosques and a number of Hindu and Buddhist temples, plus the Sanctuary of Glory where Christians worship.

Al-Hana Mosque is Langkawi's largest and most visited mosque. Located near the waterfront and Taman Legenda, its golden, onion-shaped domes provide an impressive sight. The remaining colour scheme is peach and cream. Erected in 1959, it features Moorish architecture and some motifs from Uzbekistan.

Wat Tham Kisap and Wat Koh Wanararm are two Buddhist temples to visit in the area. The first is impressively set in front of a limestone cliff and includes some golden Buddha statues, as well as giant cobra, cow and elephant sculptures. Wat Koh Wanararm is closer to Kuah, and is in a similar setting and off the main road. Built in 2000, it is located on Bukit Putih and features a large, golden, seated Buddha, a hall, eight

A colourful Hindu temple

A golden Buddha at Bukit Putih

stupas, gardens and a large white statue carved into the marble rock – this is Kuan Yin, Goddess of Mercy. There is another Buddhist temple in Kuah.

There are three Hindu temples, including the colourful Kisap Temple and Sri Maha Mariamman Devasthanam to the south of Kisap. The latter is dedicated to the goddess Mariamman, or Shakti, consort of Lord Shiva. Sri Subramaniar Devasthanam is located in Kuah behind the Langkawi Mall. Visitors are welcome to all the temples, but need to be respectful as well as to remove their shoes at the entrance.

Langkawi's Taoist community, many members of which originally hail from Hainan, worship at Thean Hou Temple in Taman Seri Aman just outside Kuah. The brightly coloured temple honours the deity Mazu (Sea Goddess) and is one of the biggest Taoist temples in Southeast Asia.

Places to Stay

There are several budget hotels in or near Kuah's commercial heart, often with rooms that have sea views at least on the upper floors. Most offer affordable rates except during local holidays, when they are popular with visiting Malaysians. They include the Langkawi Seaview, Bayview, Eagle Bay and Bella Vista Waterfront.

The most upmarket accommodation is at The Westin Langkawi and The St Regis Langkawi, both located along Pantai Beringin. While they both have seafronts lined by shade-giving trees, most guests choose to swim in the pools of the respective resorts. The Westin has rooms and suites in one of three blocks overlooking the resort pools. There are also 1–5-bedroom villas set in their own private estate off to one side. These include private whirlpool tubs and outdoor pools. Guests have several dining options, plus access to a fitness centre, spa and meeting facilities.

Nearby, The St Regis Langkawi is a luxury five-star property of Moorish architecture, including four private over-water villas. There are various dining and drinking options, a luxurious spa and a ballroom. The Langkawi International Convention Centre, with seating capacity for 1,200 guests, is conveniently located between the two resorts.

Langkawi Yacht Club Hotel is a 44-room boutique hotel overlooking the water at the Royal Langkawi Yacht Club.

The impressive lobby of The St Regis Langkawi

GUNUNG RAYA AND THE INTERIOR

Langkawi's highest peak, Gunung Raya, dominates the interior and is visible from many parts of Langkawi. There are good views over most of the island from the summit. The peak is surrounded by forests, *padi* fields and rubber estates, and small villages are a feature. While most visitors congregate along Langkawi's beaches, hiring a vehicle

Gunung Raya, the highest peak, is surrounded by a sea of rice fields

to explore the interior and to drive to Gunung Raya's summit is well worth the effort. Attractions in the interior include golf, forest adventures, agrotourism, nature activities including birdwatching at Gunung Raya and Darulaman Sanctuary, and village-based cultural activities. Visitors can stay in homestays among *padi* fields and at other boutique accommodation.

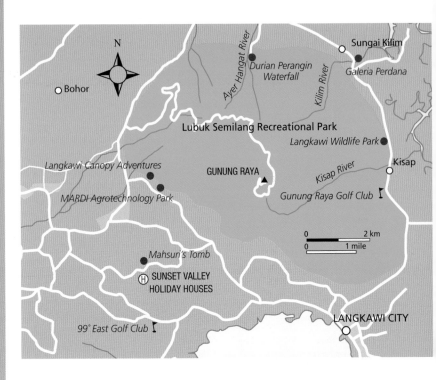

The Langkawi interior includes most of the non-coastal areas, with Gunung Raya standing tall at 881m (2,890ft). The lowlands are dominated by agricultural activity, especially *padi* rice production. The housing is quite dispersed, although there are several small villages in the interior. A large area of mostly primary forest surrounds Gunung Raya, and the road through the forest to its top is one of the best wildlife-spotting locations in Langkawi.

While driving around the interior, visitors may see locals playing a game of *sepak takraw* on a volleyball court in a village at the end of the day. The game resembles volleyball, but rather than using the hands, the feet kick a small, round rattan ball over the net. It is a very skilful game and a crowd always gathers when the best players are on a court.

Visitors can also see village football played on makeshift fields throughout the island. A popular evening activity consists of watching English Premier League football, which is screened in most coffee shops and keenly followed by many villagers.

Another common sight is people fishing in the *padi* fields. This is a very popular pastime; it is amazing just how many fish and other amphibians live in the fields.

Places to Visit

Gunung Raya (Mt Raya)

Langkawi's highest peak has impressive views over the main island and some of the surrounding islands. Local mythology has it that the mountain received its name after a fight between two families.

The mountain comprises granite rock of igneous origin. The topography is the result of volcanic activity that occurred some 140–230 million years ago, with the rock differing markedly from the surrounding sedimentary rocks. Metamorphic rocks such as marble were also formed when molten lava came into contact with the sedimentary rocks. Referred to as a granitic batholith, Gunung Raya was formed tens of millions of years ago deep beneath the Earth's surface. Subsequent tectonic movement, including the granite intrusion and erosional forces, exposed the volcanic rock at the surface.

From the main road, named Jalan Ulu Melaka, it is a 13km (8 mile), winding ascent on a sealed road all the way to the summit. The weather gets cooler with the steep ascent up the mountain, and it is a good idea to wind down the car windows in order to listen for animal sounds. A MEASAT satellite-tracking station and telecommunications facilities are located at the summit, and a small hotel once operated on the highest peak.

While most visitors drive to the summit, it is possible to walk from Lubuk Semilang Recreational Park all the way to the top via the Tangga Helang walking trail. The vegetation it traverses is interesting, but for climbers who need a distraction, count the steps as there are supposedly 4,270 in all. It is a four-hour climb – use an

Enjoy Gunung Raya's elevated views

experienced nature guide and seek advice before heading off on the trail, as it is used infrequently and is not fully maintained.

An easier alternative is to be dropped at the summit and take a leisurely walk down the road to the bottom. Early in the morning is a good time (7.00 a.m. to 10.00 a.m.) as the bird and other animal life is most active then.

Birdwatchers come in search of hornbills, especially the Great Hornbill, one of the biggest birds living on the island (measuring 1.2m/4ft from beak-tip to tail). Keep an eye out for fruit trees, which attract all hornbills. Other birds to see on the mountain include Wreathed and Oriental Pied Hornbills, Orange-breasted Flowerpeckers, woodpeckers, bulbuls, babblers and kingfishers. As the day warms up and air thermals develop, raptors such as Mountain Hawk-Eagles, White-bellied Sea Eagles and Brahminy Kites can been seen soaring above the forest.

Oriental Pied Hornbills

Forests cover much of this part of Langkawi within Gunung Raya Forest Reserve, extending over more than 5,000ha (12,355 acres). Few visitors venture up to Gunung Raya, so there is little traffic on the road. There are several lookout points where it is possible to pull over, admire the view and look for wildlife.

The cool of the early evening as the sun starts setting on the horizon is another good time to visit Gunung Raya for the birdlife, as well as for flying foxes and flying squirrels. The Crab-eating Macaque is common, while the Dusky Leaf Monkey is less commonly seen.

The slightly cooler weather on the mountain encourages some different plant species, with tree ferns commonly seen.

Langkawi Canopy Adventure

This is one of Malaysia's most unique outdoor adventure activities – thrill-seeking visitors pass through the rainforest canopy high above the forest floor, for an adrenalin-charged experience like no other. It is run by Malaysia's longest operating zipline company. The exciting but somewhat arduous activity in the heat and humidity is both thrilling and safe, as it is operated by experienced professionals on Gunung Raya.

The half-day activity starts with a resort pick-up for all participants, and transfer to the Lubuk Semilang departure point. From here, it is a 716-step walk up through the undulating terrain and primary rainforest that thrives on the mountainside. After a comprehensive training session, the adventure begins. The zipline activity features a 150m (492ft) slide along metal cables that resembles a flying fox. Participants also walk across high-wire bridges, abseil and take a 30m (98ft) vertical rappel from an emergent rainforest tree.

While this is hot and sweaty work, it is adventurous and provides an opportunity to enjoy the rainforest ecosystem. You can opt for the full experience or a lighter journey that especially appeals to families and young children. No previous skills are needed but participants should wear proper covered footwear.

Adrenalin-charged rainforest action

MARDI Agrotechnology Park

Agriculture is important for Malaysia, and the Malaysian Agricultural Research and Development Institute (MARDI) conducts research and development in various parts of the country, including Langkawi. Fruit trees grown here include the guava, mango, rambutan, durian, jackfruit and mangosteen, and visitors can sample and buy fruits. They can also explore the 14.2ha (35 acre)-site, see the views from an open-sided truck, join jungle treks and participate in other activities. There is a shop and food stall, and there is an entry fee. The farm is open daily (except Friday) from 8.30 a.m. to 5.00 p.m.

Enjoy native fruits at MARDI

Darulaman Sanctuary

This beautiful nature sanctuary is located within the Gunung Raya area, in a gazetted forest reserve that is the only one of its kind in Langkawi. It is locally managed with a strong focus on ecotourism and education. Specialist naturalists conduct nature tours with an emphasis on birds, spiders and butterflies. Nature visits are bookable in advance with choices of birdwatching, butterfly spotting or night walks. The sanctuary is highly recommended for those who appreciate flora and fauna, or just want to experience a walk in natural surroundings.

Makam Mahsuri (Mahsuri's Tomb)

Musicians at Mahsuri's Tomb

The legendary nineteenth-century Langkawi Princess Mahsuri (p. 16) was buried in what is a typical Malay village, Kampung Mawat. A white marble tomb and giant sculptured kris (dagger) are located here. There are souvenir shops and food stalls nearby. Traditional gamelan music is performed every day. The mausoleum, located off Jalan Padang Matsirat, some 12km (7.5 miles) from Kuah, is open daily from 8.00 a.m. to 6.00 p.m., and there is a small entry fee.

Learn about a local legend at Mahsuri's Tomb

Sports Facilities

99 East Golf Club (the former Langkawi Island Golf Club) is centrally located along Jalan Padang Matsirat in Kampung Mat Ayer, just 10km (6.2 miles) south-east of the airport. The current nine-hole course (destined to be 18 holes when completed) is part of a large golf and residential estate that is being developed here.

Designed by Australian golf architect Ross Wilson, the 7,330m (2,443yd) course is challenging but fair to recreational golfers. While based on a Scottish links course with wild grasses and reeds lining the fairways, it also features local design elements, including rice terraces set against rainforest backdrops. It is scenic, with distant views of Kuah and Gunung Machinchang. Facilities include a pro shop, small clubhouse, well-stocked wine cellar and highly acclaimed Fat Frog Restaurant overlooking the first hole.

Langkawi International Shooting Range (LISRAM) is just a few kilometres to the east of Gunung Raya but is only accessible via a road that leads up from Kuah. The range was used for the shooting events during the Commonwealth Games hosted by Malaysia in 1998.

Golf with views

Places of Worship

All the small villages in the Langkawi interior have mosques. Two with impressive architecture include Masjid Jamek A'Ishah and the mosque at Kampung Temoyong. Muslim worshippers pray five times a day – just before sunrise, midday, mid-afternoon, sunset and later in the evening. Villagers are called to pray by the *muezzin*, with the call usually amplified by speakers mounted in a minaret in the mosque. Mosques are busiest during the midday prayers on Friday, and visitors should avoid such times unless they just want to witness the activity from afar.

Places to Stay

Most of the accommodation is in small, owner-operated properties. Visitors can choose to stay in boutique properties such as Sunset Valley Holiday Houses, which is a collection of six traditional Malay houses relocated to a tranquil site surrounded by *padi* fields between the airport and Kuah.

Serambi Boutique Resort Home is a private, quiet, owner-operated boutique resort home in a rural setting with mountain views and a 15m (49ft) pool, just 10 minutes from Pantai Cenang.

Traditional accommodation at Sunset Valley

Outlying Islands

Pulau Dayang Bunting

This is the second largest island in the archipelago. Sited due south of the main island and at its narrowest crossing, it is just 1km (0.6 miles) across Bass Harbour from the Royal Langkawi Yacht Club. Its main visitor attractions are Tasik Dayang Bunting (Lake of the Pregnant Maiden), simple accommodation and some limestone caves.

Marble occurs on the northwestern side of the island, following metamorphic activity resulting from igneous rocks being thrust against limestone outcrops, and parts of the island are recognized as Dayang Bunting Marble Geoforest Park. Most of the island is forested, with numerous, impressive limestone outcrops including near-vertical rock walls.

A stream in the south-east snakes its way down from the highest part of the island to the narrow waterway in the east between Pulau Dayang Bunting and Pulau Tuba. Extensive stands of mangroves line the narrow waterway between the two islands. There is a bridge over the narrow waterway between Pulau Dayang Bunting and Pulau Tuba.

Tasik Dayang Bunting (Lake of the Pregnant Maiden)

This large lake on the southwestern side of the island is important in local mythology as well as to the geological world. It is documented as Lake Guillemard in some references – Sir Laurence Nunns Guillemard was the British Commissioner to Malaya in 1920–1927. Local mythology suggests that childless maidens who bathe in the lake will conceive sometime afterwards. Others suggest that the island is so named because it resembles a

Explore the waterways and caves on Dayang Bunting Island

An island-hopping tour

pregnant woman lying on her back.

The island has many limestone features, including a unique suspended freshwater lake. This was formed when the roof of a large underground cave collapsed millions of years ago. The lake fills with rainwater, but a fault beneath it allows saltwater to seep into it. As a result, the water is slightly brackish. The lake is 800m (2,625ft) long, 350m (1,148ft) wide and

There are many ways to take to the water

has a maximum depth of 14m (46ft). It is situated on limestone and is surrounded by rainforest. The island is only accessible by boat and from the jetty – it is a short walk to the lake and there is an entry fee. Many people visit as part of an organized island-hopping tour that takes in other islands in the vicinity. The cool waters of the lake are popular for swimming and paddle boarding.

Facilities here include rental of solar-powered paddleboats and kayaks, plus light refreshments. Monkeys line the path from the jetty and can be persistent in demanding food, but it is unwise and ecologically unsound to encourage this; ignore them and walk on.

Island-hopping tours of varying lengths are available all year round (weather permitting) and boats depart from Teluk Baru Jetty, Pantai Tengah or the Resorts World Langkawi Marina.

Gua Langsiar
(Cave of the Banshee)

The limestone bedrock found in parts of Langkawi contains caves, including in several parts of Pulau Dayung Bunting. Stalagmites and stalactites are just two features of limestone caves, created by erosion of this type of rock. Rainwater and carbon dioxide combine to create a weak acid called carbonic acid. This slowly erodes the limestone rock and over millions of years, caves and features such as stalagmites and stalactites are formed.

Interestingly, Gua Langsiar, on the north-west side of Pulau Dayang Bunting, is home to many cave dwellers such as bats, but not to stalactites or stalagmites. Very little is known about the cave, and while many locals have a tale to tell about it, few have been there because they think it is haunted and home to a female vampire.

The cave is accessible by boat and on foot, and some climbing is required. It is a steep climb and recommended only for those who are fit, and interested in caves and the bats that dwell in them.

Places to Stay

There are few accommodation options on the island, with homestays and a small resort being available. Barkat Chalets is a highly regarded bed and breakfast where the hosts make their guests feel like family. The chalets are located at the far northern end of Kampung Selat Bagan Nyior on the eastern side of the island. At high tide, guests can swim or kayak in the waters off the property. At low tide, it is a mud flat. Water Buffalo enjoy the mudflats and adjoining mangroves too, as do a range of waterbirds, especially waders. Home-style cooking is a feature, and the accommodation is clean and comfortable, with fans to temper the temperature. The village and chalets are just a 10-minute boat journey across Bass Harbour from Kuah Jetty.

Resort Noba, just to the south of Barkat Chalets, is another modern option. There are some 20 chalets here where guests can dine, enjoy the air-conditioned accommodation and swim in a pool.

Water buffalo grazing fields in the tranquil countryside

Pulau Beras Basah
(Wet Rice Island)

This island is located just south-east of the main island and a few minutes by boat from Pantai Cenang. It is popular for those seeking a quieter beach than Pantai Cenang and is one of the stops on an island-hopping excursion.

Beachfront coconut palms and casuarinas provide protection from the sun, and the waters are generally clear. Snorkelling is a popular activity, although there is not a great deal to see (gear can be hired on the island). Macaques can be troublesome and it is wise to carry a secure bag to prevent them from taking food. Visitors should not bring food as it can be purchased from the makeshift shop here, and they should take all their rubbish back to the main island at the day's end (the island does not need any additional litter). There are no toilets on the island. Banana-boat rides, parasailing and other watersports are available.

Pulau Singa Besar
(Giant Lion Island)

Located at the south-west tip of Langkawi, Singa Besar Island has a nature park with several trails. Birds such as White-bellied Sea Eagles and Brahminy Kites often soar high here. The northern coast of the island is worth exploring by those with an interest in rocks. Geologists refer to the rocks here as the Singa Formation, which includes thin sandstone beds and dropstone horizons interbedded with dark layers of mudstone.

Hire a boat to enjoy beaches on offshore islands

Explore rocky shorelines in a kayak

Pulau Tuba

Named after a type of plant, this is one of four inhabited islands in the archipelago where visitors can experience life in a traditional fishing village. Covering 20km² (7.7mi²), it is about 5km (3 miles) from Kuah and mostly blanketed by tropical lowland rainforest. There are six villages linked by a network of rural roads, and while the authorities have provided basic services to the island, many villagers prefer to lead a traditional lifestyle and some use wells for their water.

A homestay programme enables adventurous visitors to stay with and learn from the locals. Apart from fishing, the locals are involved in agriculture (rubber plantations and *padi* fields) and rearing animals such as chickens and Water Buffalo. Islanders source produce from the forest, including medicinal herbs, wild fruits and honey. Women supplement the household income by weaving *pandan* mats and making handicrafts. Visitors can inspect a floating fish farm situated in a secluded cove with steep limestone cliffs as a backdrop. The fish are fed and raised in the waters, and sold to restaurants.

To reach the island, visitors take a ferry from Kuah across to the fishing village located at the island's northeastern part. Boat schedules are ill defined and based on a full or near-full boat. Many visitors to the island may want to hire a motorcycle or bicycle to get around. A small bridge connects the island to neighbouring Pulau Dayang Bunting.

Places to Stay

The only island to offer accommodation is Pulau Tuba. Tuba Beach Resort and Faridzuan Motel on the northeastern coast cater to adventurous visitors. The former has rooms extending over two floors, and dormitory accommodation, a restaurant (village-style cooking) and a pool. Staff can arrange kayaks and sightseeing tours. While it is located along a tidal beach, most guests choose to swim in the resort pool. Nearby, Faridzuan Motel is a simpler property, with 13 rooms along a coconut-lined beachfront that is also tidal and a mudflat at low tide. Pulau Tuba appeals to those who like the simple things of life, especially life in a Malaysian fishing village.

Rebak Island

This island is just offshore from the main island, with its name, according to some, referring to its shape, which resembles a traditional Malay drum called a *rebak*. There are two Rebak Islands – Kecil (Small) and Besar (Big), with the island's marina and Rebak Island Resort situated on the big island just west of the small one. Both are immediately to the west of Pantai Cenang and the airport runway that extends into the bay.

Rebak Besar is a developed island that covers 138ha (390 acres), with the bulk of it bearing tropical rainforest. The deluxe resort operates a seven-minute speedboat transfer over the 2km (1.2 mile)-distance between the island and its Port Cenang terminal on the mainland, just minutes from the airport. Launch transfers begin operation at 7.15 a.m. from Rebak Island and extend through to 7.15 p.m., and from 8.15 a.m. until 7.45 p.m. from Port Cenang.

Rebak Island has one resort and a marina

Guests who want to stay longer to enjoy a meal along Pantai Cenang or its limited nightlife can arrange with resort staff to organize a private transfer outside normal hours, at a cost. Services occur roughly every hour during the day, but it is best to confirm actual times with resort staff before travelling.

Rebak Island appeals to those who want to enjoy some peace and tranquillity without the bustle of Pantai Cenang (not that there is much of that). About

Relax on Rebak Island's sandy foreshore

Yachts from around the world moor at Rebak Marina

all that disturbs guests are approaching planes landing at the airport, as the resort and island are immediately beneath the flight path. There are a few nature trails on the island, and the flora and fauna is interesting, with sightings of monkeys, hornbills, kingfishers and monitor lizards being reasonably common.

A Sailor's Haven

Apart from the expansive resort, the only other development on Rebak Island is a marina, which offers protection to yachts and a place for boat owners to do their own repairs.

The 189 wet-berth marina and adjoining resort are on the southwestern side of the island. There are good dry facilities for do-it-yourself repairs or fouling maintenance on a boat. The facilities include a 65-ton lift access for repairing equipment and 70 dry berths. Boats of up to 30m (98ft) can be accommodated, with a low-tide water depth of 2.5m (8.2ft). However, the channel opening into the marina is narrow and requires careful navigation.

Places to Stay

One island, one resort – Rebak Island Resort is the only guest accommodation on the island. The 94-room, five-star resort with a spa expands over the south-eastern side of the island and offers various low-rise room categories, including seafront aspect and suites. Restaurants and bars serve international, Indian and Asian cuisines for the enjoyment of guests and those moored in the marina.

Most guests travel to the island to relax by the pool or in the shallow waters off the coconut-palm- and casuarina-lined beachfront. Additional resort activities include kayaking, walking along nature trails, private dinners on a moon deck and strolling along the marina boardwalk. The resort's aspect results in the sunrise here being better than the sunset.

Diving at Pulau Payar

Pulau Payar serves as one of the most popular sea attractions for anyone visiting Langkawi, located 19 nautical miles (35km) south of the island. Designated as a marine park, four islands make up the Pulau Payar Marine Park – Pulau Kaca, Pulau Lembu, Pulau Segantang, and the largest, Pulau Payar.

It is the high diversity of the marine life here that attracts visitors to the marine park, and the place does get crowded at weekends and during the peak season. Visitors have to travel about 45–90 minutes depending where they depart from, and day trips are the most common option.

Sea activities include swimming, snorkelling and scuba diving, available from most travel and tour agents around Langkawi. Packages for these activities are usually all-inclusive, including return boat trips, meals, snorkelling and diving equipment, English-speaking guides and insurance. There are two main options for trips to the marine park – the standard common tours lead you to a special floating pontoon, or to the marine park beach on the main island.

For scuba divers, the Pulau Payar Marine Park is the best diving location in Langkawi. It is open to all classes of diver, and even for Discover Scuba Diving (DSD) experiences. Underwater visibility is about 5–20m (16–65ft) and depends on the season; diving depth averages around 15–25m (49–82ft). Currents are hardly experienced unless you go deeper or out into the blue – which should be avoided by beginner divers.

There are seven popular commercial dive sites here, namely: House Reef, Coral Garden, Sunken Boat Point, Grouper

Pulau Payar offers an enjoyable underwater experience

Anemonefish patrol an anemone

Farm, Sponge Reef, Lembu Rocks and Shark Point. Seasoned divers should talk to a dive operator about more advanced scuba diving, as there are a number of specialized dive sites catering to this.

Notable large and macro marine life can be seen. Among medium to large fish expect schools of snappers and trevally, and barracudas, groupers, batfish, turtles, eels, sharks, rays, pufferfish and the occasional trigger fish, which divers should be cautious about as they are territorial. Among small reef fish and macro life, you can see many colourful coral fish, clown fish, moray eels, scorpionfish, frogfish, squid, shrimps and a number of nudibranchs (sea slugs). You may even encounter a seahorse or two – these fish hide in fan corals.

The reef structure is, of course, very interesting, and divers can see various types of soft and hard coral depending on the depths they dive to. Anemones greet you when you descend at the start, and as you make your way through a dive site, table corals, sponges, and tree and fan corals can easily be seen.

For those interested in getting their scuba-diving open-water certification here, a number of companies offer a three-day PADI open-water scuba diving course. Anyone who wants to expand their scuba-diving licence from open water to advanced open water, or even take the rescue diver course, can do so here.

The best time to experience scuba diving at Pulau Payar is during the dry season in December–April, when underwater visibility is at its best. However, you can scuba dive here throughout the year as there is no off season, but the chances of spotting marine life may vary from the peak diving season.

For scuba diving at Pulau Payar Marine Park, a number of dive operators work from Kuah and along Pantai Cenang. They offer various types of scuba diving packages, either standard or tailor made. Divers can also enquire at any resort or hotel tour desk about snorkelling or diving trips.

Standard dive packages include two boat dives and additional fees for extra dives. It is always recommended that visitors use reputable licensed dive operators for any scuba diving in Langkawi.

Snorkellers may see turtles in the shallows

PART 3: THE WILDLIFE OF LANGKAWI

Langkawi Island is home to an abundance of flora and fauna due to the incredible biological diversity of the inland, mangrove and coastal forests found all over the island. The flora and fauna comprise more than 245 bird species, including nine species

Mangrove forests are a valuable habitat lining Langkawi's foreshore, especially in the north

of hornbill, 40 mammal species, including 20 bats, 30 snake species, more than 500 butterfly species, and an abundance of flowers and trees.

There are 76 mangrove plant species, 32 of which are exclusive and 33 non-exclusive, and 11 associate mangrove species; these make up almost half of the world's mangrove total. While visiting the mangroves, visitors should look out for the unique Cannonball Mangrove (*Xylocarpus granatum*) fruit in the mahogany family (Meliaceae), with its enormous fruit.

About 130 fern species are found throughout the island, ranging from lowland to montane species, as well as more than 40 orchid species, including the wild ones that grow in the rainforest and at the Geoparks. A visit to the Langkawi Orchid Farm will introduce you to a worldwide collection of orchid species (p. 59).

Anywhere on the island, flora grows openly and in abundance, dominating almost 70 per cent of the island. Visitors can spot the unique Cliff Cycad (*Cycas clivicola*) growing on the soft limestone rocks at the Kilim Geopark.

Langkawi's flora is distributed over approximately two-thirds of the island. It comprises semi-evergreen rainforests made up of lowland, heath, littoral and mangrove forests, and forest on limestone. Two mountain ranges occupy a major portion of the rainforests, while the central part of the island is relatively flat with some lower hills. Visitors are always just a short distance from the many rainforest reserves, notably the Gunung Raya Forest Reserve, Bukit Malut Forest Reserve and the ascent to Gunung Machinchang.

Fauna is popular with visitors who want to see animals in the wild, and the best places to do so are the forest reserves and any of the major mangrove areas in the

A Jurassic Cliff Cycad growing on a limestone hill

A kaleidoscope of butterflies

Birdwatchers will be attracted to the 245 bird species on the island, including the Brown-winged Kingfisher (*Halcyon amauroptera*), which is endemic to Malaysia and is easily spotted in the mangrove wetlands.

Langkawi Island is one of the up-and-coming, world-renowned butterfly enthusiasts' destinations due to the concentration of more than 500 butterfly species here. They can easily be seen at popular forest reserves; a highly recommended place in this respect is the Darulaman Sanctuary, which has a unique natural butterfly trail.

Geopark. Most major resorts have their own in-house naturalists who offer guided tours or jungle walks to see plants and animals around the island. Some resorts also offer night walks, taken at dusk, for experiencing the nocturnal wildlife such as (in some areas) the Colugo. Tours can be easily arranged with a resort's tour counter, and both private and group tours are available.

Because Langkawi is home to one of the richest mangrove communities in Malaysia, nature excursions to these wetlands are highly popular throughout the island. Visitors can book tours with specialized mangrove or wetland naturalists through their hotel or resort, or at any travel or tour agent on the island. The mangrove ecosystem boasts a high biodiversity of fauna and an equally good amount of flora that can easily be seen with the naked eye. While participating in guided mangrove tours, a visit to some of the caves can introduce you to the unique flora and fauna inside them, including bats, insects and cave plants.

Popular Places for Flora and Fauna
There is an abundance of flora and fauna throughout the island. These are three of the popular places to visit.
1. Kilim Karst Geoforest Park
2. Darulaman Sanctuary
3. Bukit Malut Forest Reserve

A fruiting Cannonball Mangrove

Habitats

There are five main habitats throughout the island – mangroves, coastal wetlands, lowlands, submontane and marine – catering to a wide diversity of flora and fauna.

Swamps and wetlands tend to be found in the south, north-east and north. The latter are mostly in the Kilim Geoforest Park, which is popular among ecotourists, and are known as mangrove forests or tidal forests.

Mangroves are the most visited natural habitat in Langkawi and are a must for anyone who is travelling to Malaysia for the first time. Mangroves are a unique ecosystem for marine life, and are very high in biodiversity for both flora and fauna. Notable and popular mangroves to visit are the Kilim Geoforest Park, Kisap Forest Reserve and Kubang Badak BioGeoTrail.

Mangrove trees in the form of an island

Coastal wetlands are permanently or seasonally flooded by water and serve a number of important functions, including water purification and storage, processing of carbon and other nutrients, stabilization of shorelines, and support for plants and animals. The coastal wetlands

The trail at Darulaman Sanctuary

in Langkawi are generally around the main mangrove systems, while other wetlands include *padi* fields.

Lowland forests are much more tropical and easier to explore on foot, and there are many lowland forest areas on the island. Flora and fauna are highly prevalent in this habitat, and include many butterflies and birds. Notable and popular areas include Pulau Dayang Bunting in the south, Machinchang in the north-west, and Gunung Raya and Darulaman Sanctuary in the centre.

Submontane forests comprise mainly mixed dipterocarp submontane forests and are located at about 700m (2,300ft) above sea level. Although they are not purely montane, traces of flora and fauna that thrive at higher elevations can be found here. A good place for them is

The cable car station on Gunung Machinchang

View of the mangrove wetlands

the Machinchang Cambrian Geoforest Park in the north-west. You can take the Panorama cable car to the top station and explore the area.

Marine habitats It is often thought that the open sea is where you find an abundance of marine habitats, but the amazing mangrove system in Langkawi is also home to an incredible array of marine species, providing nesting and breeding habitats for fish, shellfish, migratory birds and even sea turtles. Recommended places to experience this type of habitat are the mangrove wetlands and Pulau Payar Marine Park (p. 90).

What are Wetlands?

According to the Ramsar Convention, which was launched in 1971, wetlands are an 'area of marsh, peat land, fen or water, whether natural or artificial, permanent or temporary, with water that is static, flowing, fresh, brackish or salt, including areas of marine water, the depth of which at low tide does not exceed six metres'. While academics have been arguing about what defines a wetland, it also goes by many other names, such as swamps, peatland, sloughs, marshes, muskegs, bogs, fens, potholes and mires.

Wildlife Reserve in Langkawi

The wildlife reserve in Langkawi at Pulau Singa Besar (Big Lion Island) is in the south-west of the main island. Here you can find wildlife that is spread over 11.3km² (2,792 acres), including macaques, monitor lizards, snakes, geckos, birds including hornbills, mouse-deer, otters, bats and Wild Boar.

The island was set up as a bird and other wildlife sanctuary in 1988 and currently there is no accommodation available apart from a campsite. For nature lovers, there are four main trails, and there is a wildlife park staff quarters. Daily boat tours to the island depart from Kuah Jetty. You can ask any local tour agent about day trips or camping trips to the island.

Lowland Forests

In Langkawi Island, lowland forests grow on flat land at generally less than 1,000m (3,300ft), and are divided into primary and secondary lowland forests. They are known as one of the most complex, dense and species-rich forests in the world, with a climate that is continuously warm and humid.

Lowland rainforests contain some unique regional flora and fauna specific to only this part of the world, and visitors can see them without travelling deep into the forests. The vast diversity of the lowland forests is also an important contribution to the overall rainforest ecosystem.

Lowland forests are scattered throughout the main island and also on some of the smaller islands. They can be visited via guided tours with credible naturalists through nature walks, hikes and treks. Specialized wildlife, butterfly watching and birdwatching tours are available from reputable nature

tour companies. Among some of the recommended places to explore is the new Darulaman Sanctuary in Lubuk Semilang, in the centre of Langkawi and at the foot of Gunung Raya. This secondary forest, 91.4ha (226 acre)-reserve boasts an experiential two-hour nature walk aimed at learning and understanding the flora and fauna of the area. Along the nature walk, visitors are greeted by centuries-old hardwood trees and more than 100 medicinal plants on the main trail. While exploring the flora, various insects, butterflies and birds can easily be seen.

Pasir Tengkorak Eco Forest Park in the north-east is a coastal lowland forest worth visiting. It combines both the beach and coastal forest with different flora species unlike those commonly found in the general lowland rainforest. The forest park is a commercial type of place, with park benches, picnic areas and white sandy beaches, and is open from 7.00 a.m. to 6.00 p.m. daily with no entrance fees.

On a trek in the forest

Second layer of the rainforest canopy

Visitors can self-drive to access it.

The Datai Bay area is an exclusive rainforest that also has its own coastal lowland forest, but not everyone has open access to it as it houses two of the most luxurious resorts – The Datai and The Andaman Resorts, which are next to each other. Most of the ecotourism experiences here are conducted through the resorts' in-house naturalists or by booking specialized rainforest tours from selected nature-tour companies in Langkawi.

Overall, flora and fauna make up the main highlights for visits to lowland forests, where primates, squirrels, slow lorises, civet cats, birds, insects, tropical shrubs, flowering plants, and more than 2,000 tree species thrive. Because wildlife spotting is always a matter of chance, visitors should note that rainforests are not zoos, and seeing certain wildlife is always a matter of luck. Flowering plants and fruits are seasonal, so there are certain times in the year when some flowers will bloom or trees will bear fruits. It is always best to ask a naturalist or nature guide about what can be seen at the time of a visit.

Tree Canopies

There are three layers of tree canopy in a lowland forest.

1. The lower layer canopy is made up of saplings of a number of species.
2. The second layer canopy is at 23–30m (75–98ft).
3. The upper layer canopy towers at 30–40m (98–130ft), with occasional giants reaching 60m (177ft).

Wetlands

The coastal wetlands, or mangroves, are one of the main attractions to ecotourism, and they spread all the way from the south between Pulau Tuba and Pulau Dayang Bunting, to the north-east rivers, Ayer Hangat, Kisap and the famous Kilim River. What makes the coastal wetlands in Langkawi special is the fact that the mangrove forest coincides with the lowland forest, and visitors get to experience both the diverse wetlands and the Geopark that showcases wondrous karst rock formations. In an unofficial calculation, there are an estimated 8,000ha (20,000 acres) of mangrove wetlands throughout Langkawi, and in recent years there has been much debate over the speedy development of tourism in these particular Geopark areas and the effect it may have.

The coastal wetlands contain a wide range of flora and fauna, with an estimated 62 mangrove species, a fairly large variety of wetland birds, mangrove crabs, mudskippers, lobsters, reptiles like mangrove snakes and lizards, and the occasional macaques.

Boats ready to tour the Kilim River wetlands

One of the unique coastal wetland experiences involves taking a boat tour to see how the ecosystem thrives in different conditions, and also how the tide plays an important role for both flora and fauna.

Countless wetland or mangrove tours are available at commercial areas on the island. However, you should take note of the different tour types being offered – budget mangrove tours usually include the unethical practice of eagle and macaque feeding. They usually do not include a tour guide and are operated by local boatmen who take tourists to

Macaques inhabit the mangroves

popular feeding spots. Often, these tours are branded as wildlife spotting. Tours usually end by stopping at some of the local floating fishing farms located along the mangroves. Visitors are treated to a feeding showcase of many different marine fish that live in makeshift holding areas, some for show and others for breeding. The floating fish farms double as floating restaurants that sell local seafood and drinks to visitors. Various boat-tour packages include meals that may be taken at these fish farms.

There are options for ethical wetland tours, where choices include guided private or shared tours available from a number of reputable tour companies, and the prices vary quite a bit.

Guided mangrove tours usually last for 2–5 hours depending on the package selected, and prices are based on either per person or per boat. Most groups or families usually opt to book an entire boat for a tour.

Marine Ecosystems

Pulau Payar Marine Park is the only marine park in Langkawi and also the oldest marine park in Malaysia, set up in 1994. It is the only pristine coral reef on the entire west coast of Malaysia, with a rich marine life and diversity of corals and coral fish. Visitors can spot various wildlife, including birds, mammals and corals, in just one place. The marine ecosystem applies not only to the general sea, however, but also to the estuaries and mangrove wetlands, where there is a high marine biodiversity.

In Langkawi, the general marine ecosystems are threatened daily by mass tourism, and this being a highly popular tourist location, the authorities have been working hard to keep the marine ecosystem protected in all ways possible. It has also been under threat from overfishing and global warming, and there has been much research by the local authorities, including the Geopark authorities, in the last decade into countering and fixing the immediate issues.

Various academics have been stressing the importance of Marine Protected Areas (MPAs), which provide perhaps the best way of preserving the existing complexity of the marine habitat, and preventing the decline or collapse of the ecosystem. Currently, Malaysia has about 2.3 per cent of marine area under protection, indicating that more must be done to meet international targets and standards. For now, visitors to the island can enjoy the marine ecosystem at Langkawi Coral, which is a specially built floating platform that moves around the Pulau Payar Marine Park. This massive pontoon also serves as an underwater observatory with a special glassed viewing area, and offers

The floating diving centre at Pulau Payar Marine Park.

A local fishing village beach

swimming, snorkelling and some scuba diving that employs strong ecotourism ethics.

Motorized sea sports like jet skiing and parasailing have been contributors to negative impacts on marine conservation, and most beaches around Langkawi have banned these activities. Only a couple of beaches still practise them, at Pantai Cenang due to its popularity among the mass tourists.

As always, visitors are reminded to book reputable and recognized tour operators in order to contribute to maintaining the marine ecosystem. Their highly trained naturalists or specialized guides know how to explain the importance of the ecosystem; in return, visitors get a proper education about marine conservation.

Geology

Geologically, Langkawi consists of mainly sandstone with a high iron content, which is why some claim that the name Langkawi comes from this. 'Lang' is the abbreviation of helang, the Malay name for eagle, and *'kawi'* means red sandstone. When put together, the name sounds like 'Red Sandstone Eagle'. Langkawi enjoys UNESCO Global Geopark status, which comes as no surprise considering the fact that some of its rock formations are more than 550 million years old, and the oldest in Southeast Asia.

The island's geological landscape comprises five key rock formations, known as Machinchang, Setul, Singa, Chuping and the igneous rock of Gunung Raya, which have given rise to local legends. These are found in the popular tourist areas of

Local fishing and commercial boats moored at the Tanjung Rhu beach

Geology of Langkawi Timeline

1. Machinchang Formation (Early–Late Cambrian).
2. Setul Formation (Early Ordovician–Middle Devonian).
3. Singa Formation (Late Devonian–Late Early Permian).
4. Chuping Formation (Early Permian–possibly Late Triassic).
5. Granite (Late Triassic).

A rock formation with fossilized shells

Gunung Machinchang, Gunung Raya and Belanga Pecah (Battle of the Giants of Mat Chinchang and Mat Raya), Gua Cerita (Legend of the Roman Emperor's Son and mythical giant bird) and Pulau Dayang Bunting (Tale of a Pregnant Maiden).

The south and east consist mainly of limestone and siltstone mixtures, and the centre, where Gunung Raya is located, consists of granite and limestone with parts of basalt. The soft limestone and sea erosion are the main reasons why there are caves at the southern, eastern and northern parts of the island.

Langkawi marble is a world-famous product of the island. It is mined in the east and south, and exported around the world. The marble has a mild reddish tone, which is due to its heavy iron content.

There are unique black-sand beaches in the north of Langkawi (p.50). This phenomenon is a result of a mixture of minerals – ilmenite, tourmaline and zirconium – occurring in layers and being washed up by sea currents and monsoon waves. Those interested in geology can take specialized tours to visit some of the places that are of interest.

Langkawi and Global Geoparks

The Global Geopark Network (GGN) was originally established in 1998. It was partly supported by UNESCO until 2015, and was officially designated as UNESCO Global Geoparks in the same year. As of 2019, there are a total of 147 Global UNESCO Geoparks in 41 countries around the world.

The Langkawi Geopark is the first in Malaysia and also in Southeast Asia (which only has six Geoparks); this has made the island one of the most popular places to visit in Malaysia. The Geopark is an astounding 550 million years old, which is quite a feat from this part of the world. Getting the UNESCO Global Geopark title was not easy. The Kedah Government initially submitted a proposal in 2001, and in May 2006 Langkawi was renamed Langkawi Geopark by the state government in order to obtain the

UNESCO status. The Langkawi UNESCO Global Geopark comprises four main areas: the Machinchang Cambrian Geoforest Park, Kilim Karst Geoforest Park, Dayang Bunting Marble Geoforest Park and Kubang Badak BioGeoTrail, the latter being a recent addition. The Geopark is in the northeastern part of Langkawi, where some of the finest examples of intriguing rock formations are located.

A Geopark is not, however, solely about rock formations. It focuses on the local communities within it that sustain and nurture the geological heritage through effective conservation efforts and promotion of ecotourism.

The oldest rock formation in Malaysia is in the Datai Bay area. It is known as the Machinchang Formation, created out of inter-bedded sandstone and shale. The

Entrance to the Dayang Bunting Marble Forest Geopark

An aerial view of the rock formation at Datai Bay

UNESCO Global Geoparks in Southeast Asia

There are only ten UNESCO Global Geoparks in Southeast Asia.

1. Langkawi Global Geopark, Kedah, Malaysia.
2. Satun Global Geopark, southern Thailand.
3. Batur Global Geopark, Indonesia.
4. Ciletuh-Palabuhanratu Global Geopark, Indonesia.
5. Gunung Sewu Global Geopark, Indonesia.
6. Rinjani-Lombok Global Geopark, Indonesia.
7. Toba Caldera Global Geopark, Sumatra, Indonesia.
8. Dak Nong Global Geopark, Central Highlands, Vietnam.
9. Dong Van Karst Plateau, Ha Giang Province, Vietnam.
10. Non Nuoc Cao Bang Geopark, Cao Bang Province, Vietnam.

Viewpoint at the top of the cable car station at Gunung Machinchang

corner of Langkawi. Gunung Raya, the tallest mountain range on the island, stands at 881m (2,890ft). The Machinchang range is the oldest rock formation on Langkawi and Malaysia, standing 713m (2,339ft) above sea level at the main peak. Created over half a billion years ago, it is claimed by experts that this was the first part of Southeast Asia to rise from the sea bed during the Cambrian Period.

Kilim Geoforest Park

In the north-east is the rugged karst limestone terrain called the Kilim

Floating fish farms at the Kilim Geoforest Park

formation dates back 550 million years and is a key area for conservation and research purposes.

Receiving the UNESCO title is not a lifelong designation. Every four years, UNESCO sends its officers to reassess the status and ensure that proper UNESCO guidelines are being followed. There are ten compulsory focus areas that a Geopark must follow in order to be renewed: natural resources, geological hazards, climate change, education, science, culture, women, sustainable development, local and indigenous knowledge, and geoconservation.

Machinchang Mountain Ranges and Gunung Raya

These are located in the northwestern

Geoforest Park, which is surrounded by numerous rivers that wind through vast mangrove forest. The main river is known as Sungai Kilim. Here ecotourism is at its best, offering visitors numerous eco-activities via fibreglass boats that cater to all kinds of mangrove tours, including eagle spotting, cave visits and overall mangrove wildlife spotting. Along the journey, visitors get to see astonishing limestone formations that took millions of years of erosion to form. Most of the general mangrove and nature tours in Langkawi are conducted at the Kilim Geoforest Park.

Dayang Bunting Geopark

In the south of Langkawi Island is Dayang Bunting Island that, according to legend, is famous for a freshwater lake known as the Lake of the Pregnant Maiden. This unique lake originated as a massive limestone cave that collapsed to create what it is today. The place is highly popular as a tourist destination due to the folk legend, according to which a princess who lost her newborn baby and buried the infant in the lake then blessed the waters with fertility. Couples who have trouble conceiving make their way here to swim in the waters. When you look at the island from

a certain angle, you can see the shape of a pregnant maiden lying on her back. Other notable features include one of the finest Permian marble formations in the world, from which the famous Langkawi Marble is extracted by mining.

Kubang Badak BioGeo Trail

This is the latest location, added to the Langkawi UNESCO Global Geopark in 2018, making up the four main Geopark locations. It offers visitors pristine mangroves, geological diversity and the distinctive cultural history of the Siamese settlers who migrated here more than 200 years ago. The name Kubang Badak translates as watering hole for a hippopotamus, which appears a little strange as the animal is not native to Malaysia. The place also includes a 490ha (1,210 acre)-mudflat and mangrove swamp that features among 13 places of

Jetty at the Kubang Badak BioGeo Trail

interest in north-west Langkawi.

Some of the areas to explore here are Jemuruk Island, where you can see fossils of prehistoric trilobites, Dangli Island for its rich marine life and corals, Tanjung Buta for the massive mangrove mudflats, Kampung Siam for the centuries-old charcoal factory, and the Pinang Cave for its unique limestone karst, fossilized shells and largest concentration of bats in Langkawi. Visitors usually start their journey from the main Kubang Badak jetty.

Langkawi Geopark Ethical Practices

As at all UNESCO World Heritage Sites and UNESCO Global Geoparks, there are strict practices that everyone, including visitors, should follow.

1. **Littering** Do not leave your rubbish behind; be considerate, pick up any rubbish lying around and place it into a proper dustbin.

2. **Smoking** Do not smoke at any of the Geopark locations. If you must, check with a local guide or the authorities whether there is a smoking area.

3. **Feeding Wildlife** This has become a hot topic in Langkawi, with some unethical guides and tourists having been seen feeding the wildlife just to take photos. By doing this, they are disrupting the ecological cycle and becoming a contributor as a bad tourist – so do not do it.

4. **Swimming and Diving** Some Geopark locations offer swimming or scuba diving. Be careful around the coral reefs. Standing on them damages the corals and also harms the ecology of marine wildlife.

Photographic Identification Guide to the Wildlife of Langkawi

The following pages are an introductory identification guide to commonly seen, and significant animals and plants to be found on Langkawi. For each species, the text gives the common name, scientific name and size. The size indicates the body length. For some the local name is also included. The descriptions cover identifying features, diet and where the species can be seen.

Mammals

Sunda Pangolin
Manis javanica 40–65cm
(Pengulling)

Generally larger and lighter in colour that other pangolin species. Short foreclaws that are thick and powerful to dig into soil in search of ants' nests or tear into termite mounds. Body covered by rows of scales and fibrous hair. Weighs up to 10kg. Male larger than female. The Malay word *pengguling*, means 'one who rolls up'. Considered Critically Endangered. Rarely seen.

Common Tree Shrew
Tupaia glis lacernata 16–21cm

Varying colours of reddish-brown, greyish or black upperparts and whitish belly. Long, bushy tail dark greyish-brown and almost reaches length of body. Very active by day and found in small to large trees. Standard diet includes fruits, seeds, leaves and insects, especially ants, spiders and small lizards. Found in most resort grounds and even in commercial areas but not very easy to spot.

Sunda Colugo
Galeopterus variegatus 33–42cm

Nocturnal animal popular among wildlife enthusiasts. Common in Datai area but less so at Pantai Pasir Tenkorak. Lives in small groups and often territorial when it comes to sleeping areas. Completely arboreal. Instead of flying, it glides from tree to tree, reaching more than 100m in distance. Diet includes leaves, flowers, shoots, buds and sap. Langkawi is one of the easiest places to see colugos in Malaysia.

Crab-eating Macaque
Macaca fascicularis 38–55cm
(Long-tailed Macaque)

The long tail adds another 40–65cm. Commonly seen all over the island and travels in packs of 3–20. Known to live alongside humans here. Easily seen at mangroves, caves and occasionally in commercial areas near a rainforest. Often seen while driving along island's inner roads. Do not feed them – they can be aggressive and a health hazard.

Dusky Leaf Monkey
Trachypithecus obscurus 42–61cm
(Spectacled Langur, Spectacled Leaf Monkey, Lutung, Lutong)

Seen in lush rainforests of Langkawi. Large, white-coloured circles around eyes give appearance of spectacles. White-coloured patches of fur around mouth and stomach. Newborns orange or yellow in colour. Travels in groups and are active by day in higher canopies. Generally shy of human interaction.

Wild Boar
Sus scrofa 110–150cm
(Banded Pig)

Rare in Langkawi, though can be sighted. Probably originated in Southeast Asia during Early Pleistocene Period. Adult boars vary from grey to black to reddish-brown. Juveniles brownish with distinctive horizontal stripes. Forages mainly on young shoots, worms, roots, tubers and plantation crops; while in mangroves feeds on carrion, arthropods and molluscs. Easiest to see in Datai Bay area (visitors have seen it at the beach).

Water Buffalo

Bubalus bubalis 2–2.5m
(Asian Water Buffalo, Domestic Water Buffalo)

Easily spotted in *padi* fields and commercial wetlands around Langkawi. Large mammal that thrives on many aquatic plants; will eat shrubs and trees when it cannot find grass or herbs. Spends most of its time in water. Hooves extra wide, preventing it from sinking into mud at the bottoms of ponds, swamps and rivers.

Lesser Mouse-deer

Tragulus javanicus 35–45cm
(Java Mouse-deer)

Smallest hoofed mammal in the world. Very shy and rarely sighted in Langkawi; sometimes seen in Datai Bay area. Active from dusk to dawn. Diet primarily leaves, shrubs, shoots, buds and fungi, in addition to fruits that have fallen from trees. Males territorial. Also known as Sang Kancil in Malay folklore, and usually featured in stories as a quick-witted character.

Common Palm Civet

Paradoxurus musangus 42–50cm (body); 33–42cm (tail)
(Musang)

Identified by three dark stripes along the back, on a creamy or grey background. They feed mainly on fruit, being particularly attracted to mangos, but will eat worms and insects. They frequently eat the fruits of the Fishtail Palm *Caryota mitis*. They usually nest in hollow trees where they raise 2–3 young. The species is fully nocturnal.

Small-toothed Palm Civet
Arctogalidia trivirgata 50–53cm (body),
63–66cm (tail), 2–2.5kg
(Three-striped Palm Civet)

Occurs in primary rainforest and
secondary forest, is nocturnal and mainly
arboreal. Fur colour is mainly greyish
(sometimes reddish-brown), becoming
paler and yellowish around the neck
and belly. Facial fur is black and some
individuals have a narrow pale strip on the
forehead. Three dark stripes extend from
the neck to the tail base. Tail is dark and
prehensile. The civet is omnivorous.

Smooth-coated Otter
Lutrogale perspicillata 52–75cm
(Eurasian Otter)

Medium-sized otter similar to the Hairy-
nosed Otter, but with smoother and
shorter fur. Found at wetlands, seasonal
swamps, rivers, lakes, rice *padis* and
sometimes beaches around Langkawi.
Active by day and often seen in groups of
4–6, and at times up to 11. Diet includes
various fish, and during rice harvest
season hunts rats, snakes, amphibians and
insects. Not easy to see.

Oriental Small-clawed Otter
Aonyx cinerea 45–61cm
(Asian Small-clawed Otter)

Among the smallest species in the world.
Deep brown fur and pale under belly,
and brown head. Best seen at freshwater
wetlands such as swamps, meandering
rivers and irrigated rice fields, as well as
estuaries, coastal lagoons and tidal pools.
Lives in groups of up to 15 individuals.
Feeds mainly on crabs, and mudskippers
and other fish. Guidance of a naturalist is
needed to spot it in known locations around
Langkawi.

Red Giant Flying Squirrel
Petaurista petaurista 35–42cm
(Sunda Flying Lemur)

Largest of the flying squirrel family in Southeast Asia and predominantly nocturnal. Dark brown above and orange below, with black snout, black feet and black tip to tail. Diet includes conifer cones, leaves and branches, and when in season, fruits and nuts, and occasionally insects. Migrates in rainforest for food. Instead of flying, glides from tree to tree, often up to 75m. Found in Datai Bay area and in north-west parts of Langkawi.

Grey-bellied Squirrel
Callosciurus caniceps 22–30cm

One of the most common squirrels, found in a variety of habitats including primary and secondary forests, disturbed habitats, and mature parks and gardens. Upperside of body olive-brown, and belly light grey or silvery. Long tail thick with fur, sometimes with vague grey banding and black tip. Generally not shy, and may approach close to human habitation. Diet comprises fruits, seeds, flowers and insects. Easily seen throughout the island.

Black Giant Squirrel
Ratufa bicolor 35–58cm
(Malayan Giant Squirrel)

One of the largest squirrels in the world. Solitary and distinctly bicoloured, with dark upperparts and pale underparts. Back, top of head, ears and bushy tail deep brown to black; underparts orange or light buff coloured. Feeds on seeds, pine cones, fruits and leaves ranging from canopy to the ground. Found from sea level up to 1,400m. Seen in Datai Bay area, Darulaman Sanctuary and other dense lowland forest areas.

Birds

Lesser Whistling-duck
Dendrocygna javanica 38–42cm
Commonly seen in wet rice fields, these birds are widespread in South and Southeast Asia. Chestnut-brown in colour with orange-yellow ring around eye. Nocturnal bird that rests mainly in the day. Seen in freshwater wetlands with good vegetation, and sometimes in *padi* fields, but not an everyday bird to sight. Feeds mainly on water plants, as well as grain from cultivated rice, and small fish, frogs, molluscs and worms.

Purple Heron
Ardea purpurea 78–97cm
Fairly large heron, dark reddish-brown with dark grey back. Bill and legs amber and yellow. Snake-like, long neck. Seen in marshland, wetlands, ponds and *padi* fields. Usually solitary. Diet consists of fish, small mammals and amphibians, as well as nestling birds, snakes, lizards, crustaceans, water snails, insects and spiders. Widespread across Europe and Asia, and both resident and migrant through Southeast Asia.

Chinese Pond Heron
Ardeola bacchus 45–47cm
Lowland bird with special appearance of dual colours. Strikingly chestnut-brown with pure white wings during breeding season; greyish-brown flecked with white at other times. Found mainly in saltwater wetlands including mangroves and tidal pools, but also rivers, freshwater ponds and *padi* fields. Diet consists mainly of insects, small frogs, worms, fish, molluscs and crustaceans. Migratory bird from North Asia.

Great Egret
Casmerodius albus 80–104cm

One of the largest herons, with all-white plumage, yellow bill and black legs. Normally seen in wetlands, *padi* fields, ponds, lakes and sometimes mangroves. Feeds in shallow water or drier habitats, mainly on fish, frogs, small mammals, small reptiles and insects. Walks with neck extended and wings held close. Not a vocal bird.

Little Egret
Egretta garzetta 55–65cm

One of the smaller egrets in the heron family. Almost white plumage, and black beak and legs. Sociable bird, often seen in flocks around wetlands, *padi* fields, water catchments and at times in mangroves. Diet includes fish, amphibians, small reptiles, crustaceans, molluscs, insects, spiders and worms.

Cattle Egret
Bubulcus ibis 88–96cm

One of the Water Buffalo's best friends, often seen hanging around the mammals and sometimes on their backs. Usually fully white in colour with yellow bill and greyish-yellow legs. During breeding season, cinnamon-coloured back and breast, and the legs and bill flush with red. Found at most water areas, including coastal islands, and often seen with other heron and egret species. Diet includes insects, especially grasshoppers, crickets, flies, moths, spiders, frogs and earthworms.

Red-wattled Lapwing
Vanellus indicus 32–35cm

Large plover often spotted at wet grassland, marshes and well-vegetated fringes of ponds as well as *padi* fields. Red wattle in front of eyes. Wings and back light brown with a purple to green sheen and the head is black, with a prominent white patch running between these two colours, from belly to tail, flanking neck to sides of crown.

White-bellied Sea Eagle
Haliaeetus leucogaster 66–80cm
(White-breasted Sea Eagle)

Majestic bird easily seen all over Langkawi. Overall white in colour except for upperparts, which are grey, black under the tips of the wings, and yellow or grey feet. Female slightly larger than male. Generally territorial. In Langkawi, a number of them can be seen together in parts of Kilim Geopark Forest. Hunts mainly aquatic animals, such as fish, turtles and sea snakes.

Brahminy Kite
Haliasturindus 39–46cm
(Helang)

The island of Langkawi is often said to be named after the Brahminy Kite, and a massive 12m statue of this bird is located at Dataran Lang in Kuah. Easy to distinguish from other birds of prey due to reddish-brown or chestnut-coloured body plumage that contrasts with white head and breast. Known primarily as a scavenger, feeding mainly on dead fish and crabs, especially in wetlands. Often spotted near coastlines, resorts and even at higher altitudes.

Mountain Hawk-eagle
Nisaetus nipalensis 66–84cm

Breeding range from India and Nepal, to Thailand, Indonesia and Japan. Not easy to see, but a good bird guide can identify exact locations in Langkawi – the only place in Malaysia where it can be seen. Adult has brown upperparts and pale underparts, with barring on undersides of flight feathers and tail. Commonly seen on Gunung Raya at 300–500m, with best views being of bird in flight or looking for prey. Diet includes small mammals such as rodents, birds and reptiles.

Crested Goshawk
Accipiter trivirgatus 40–46cm

Uncommon. Female larger than male, which has dark brown crown, grey sides of head, and black moustachial and throat-stripes. Pale underparts patterned with rufous streaks on breast and bars on belly. Often seen in lowland forest up to hilly or lower montane areas; also in mangroves. Hunts birds, frogs, mammals and small reptiles, including lizards.

Zebra Dove
Geopelia striata 20–23cm

Common bird seen just about anywhere on the island. Plumage brownish-grey on upperparts with black-and-white barring. Underparts pinkish with black bars on sides of neck, breast and belly. Face blue-grey with bare blue skin around eyes. Feeds on small grasses, weed seeds, insects and other small invertebrates. In public areas, feeds on scraps, rice and bread, and is not shy.

Asian Koel
Eudynamys scolopaceus 39–46cm

Large, long-tailed member of cuckoo family. Male noisy. Glossy bluish-black in colour with pale green beak and grey legs. Female dark brown with white and buff spots. Both sexes have reddish eyes. Commonly seen around Langkawi and easy to distinguish by extra-loud calls. Adults feed mainly on fruits and can often be seen around palm trees during fruiting season, but diet includes insects, caterpillars, eggs and small vertebrates.

Greater Coucal
Centropus sinensis 40–48cm

Crow-like bird with long tail and coppery-brown wings. Commonly found in wide range of habitats, from jungle to cultivation and urban gardens. Cannot fly long distances and known to sunbathe in the mornings singly or in pairs on top of vegetation with wings spread out. Eats birds' eggs, nestlings, fruits, seeds, wide range of insects, caterpillars and small vertebrates. Call is a series of deep booms.

Orange-breasted Trogon
Harpactes oreskios 28–31cm

Beautiful bird that can be seen in the lower canopy of forest reserves and lower montane areas. Olive-yellow head with feathers that are bristly and upright, chestnut upperparts, orange breast and blue bill. Diet includes Orthoptera, cicadas, bugs, beetles, ants, stick insects and caterpillars. Usually very quiet.

Oriental Dollarbird
Eurystomus orientalis 28–30cm

One of the roller family. Name derives from distinctive blue, coin-shaped spots on wings. Overall colour dark brown, heavily washed with bluish-green sheen on back and wing-coverts, and glossy bright blue colouring on throat and undertail. Usually eats insects such as bugs. Most commonly seen hawking from a prominent perch. Inhabits lowland to lower montane rainforest areas.

Brown-winged Kingfisher
Pelargopsis amauroptera 32–36cm

One of eight kingfisher species seen on the island. Dark brown wings and tail, and light brown underbelly, breast and head. Bill and legs reddish-orange, and male and female are the same. Inhabits mangrove-lined rivers in northern parts of Langkawi and often hard to spot. Feeds on small fish and crabs and is a very patient hunter.

Collared Kingfisher
Todiramphus chloris 23–29cm
(Mangrove Kingfisher, White-collared Kingfisher)

Easily seen around mangroves, wetlands and coastal areas. Blue above and white below, with a white collar round back of neck. Often seen at resort grounds and also perched on electrical wires. Diet includes insects, worms, snails, shrimps, frogs, lizards, small fish and sometimes other small birds. Probably one of the most common kingfisher species in Langkawi.

White-throated Kingfisher
Halcyon smyrnensis 27–28cm
(White-breasted Kingfisher)

Bright blue back, wings and tail. Head, shoulders, flanks and lower belly chestnut, and throat and breast white. Large bill and legs bright red. Noisy during breeding season and seen from mangroves to commercial areas, on electrical wires. Feeds on wide range of prey, including small reptiles, amphibians, crabs, small rodents and even small birds. Active by day and commonly seen.

Banded Kingfisher
Lacedo pulchella 18–20cm

One of the harder species to spot. Male has bright blue crown with black and blue banding on back. Female has rufous and black banding on head and upperparts. Both have a beautiful bright red bill. Inhabits lowland forest. Diet includes large insects and occasionally small lizards. Uncommon but can be found with a bird guide.

Blue-throated Bee-eater
Merops viridis 18–21cm

One of the most colourful birds sighted in lowland forest and mangroves, and occasionally around commercial open areas on electrical cables. Known as a migratory bird from Sumatra to West Malaysia. Seen in Langkawi November–March. Colourful plumage comprising chestnut nape, dark green wings, light green breast and signature blue throat. Diet consists mostly of bees, wasps, bugs and dragonflies. Often seen in flocks.

Great Hornbill
Buceros bicornis 95–130cm

One of the largest hornbills. Can be seen in forest reserves and at Gunung Raya. Male larger than female, with red eyes; female has bluish-white eyes. Most prominent feature is bright yellow and black casque on top of massive bill, and black and white feathers on body and spread wings. Eats insects, nestling birds and small lizards, and often seen in small flocks. Highly protected bird listed as Vulnerable on IUCN Red List.

Oriental Pied Hornbill
Anthracoceros albirostris 55–60cm

Smallest of the hornbill family in Malaysia and the most commonly sighted hornbill in Langkawi. Often seen at Tanjung Rhu. Plumage of head, neck, back, wings and upper breast black with slight green sheen. Tail black with white tips on all feathers, eyes red, and bill and casque yellow. Feeds on fruits, insects, shellfish, small reptiles, and sometimes small mammals and birds, including their eggs.

Wreathed Hornbill
Rhyticeros undulatus 75–85cm

Found in primary evergreen forested foothills and up to mountain tops. Mostly black; male has yellow throat, female blue. One place where they are often spotted is around Gunung Raya. Usually feed on fruits, and during the breeding period the male hunts small creatures for both mother and chicks. Spotted in small flocks from 5–20 birds. They live for around 40-50 years.

Great Slaty Woodpecker

Mulleripicus pulverulentus 48–58cm

Largest species of woodpecker in the world. Distinctive features of very long, strong, chisel-tipped bill, elongated neck and long tail. Plumage almost entirely dark grey or blackish slate-grey overlaid with small white spots on face. Throat paler grey and males have small red moustache. Seen in small groups in primary and secondary forests. Shares feeding sites in the form of nests of social insects such as ants, termites, wood-boring beetles and stingless bees.

Blue-winged Pitta

Pitta moluccensis 18–20cm

Highly popular among birdwatchers. Very colourful with black head, buff stripe above eye, white collar, greenish upperparts, bright blue wings, buff underparts and reddish vent area. Diet includes worms and insects, which it hunts for on the ground or from a low branch or perch. Best way to see it is with a local bird guide.

Black-naped Oriole

Oriolus chinensis 23–28cm

Striking bird. Head, upperparts and underparts entirely golden-yellow, with black head-stripe broadening and joining at back of neck. Bill pink and black legs. Found widely in rainforests, gardens, plantations and resort grounds. Diet includes insects, figs and berries. Often seen singly or in pairs.

Ochraceous Bulbul
Alophoixus ochraceus 12–22cm

Brownish-olive bulbul with a wispy crest and a glowingly white, puffy throat. Inhabits lowland and foothill forests, where it prefers primary or well-aged secondary growth. Forages in the middle and lower levels of forest, usually in small, noisy flocks. Calls consist primarily of loud, dry 'chek' notes; song is pleasant and warbling.

Olive-winged Bulbul
Pycnonotus plumosus 20–25cm

Large plain bulbul of lowland forests, forest edges and mangroves. Dull brown with grey-streaked ear coverts, red eyes and olive-green panels on the wings. Other similar large brown bulbuls, such as Red-eyed, can also have olive tones in the wings but less prominently. Song is a simple series of bubbly warblings interspersed with sharper notes.

Brown-throated Sunbird
Anthreptes malacensis 12–14cm

Colourful bird seen in most places where flowers are in bloom as it loves to feed on nectar. Native to Southeast Asia. Male has iridescent green and purple upperparts with chestnut on wing-coverts. Female olive-green above and yellowish below. Feeds mainly on nectar, and small fruits including berries.

Crimson Sunbird
Aethopyga siparaja 11–15cm
One of the brightest sunbirds. Adult male has crimson breast, maroon back, yellow rump and olive belly. Female has olive-green back and yellowish breast. Feeds mainly on nectar. Very fast bird with high-pitched calls during flight. Seen in lowland to lower montane forests in Langkawi.

Olive-backed Sunbird
Cinnyris jugularis 10–11.4cm
(Yellow-bellied Sunbird)
Blue-black forehead, throat and upper breast, rufous band across breast, underparts bright yellow. Often seen in numerous places like common urban areas, mangroves, and lowland and coastal forests. Eats small insects, spiders, nectar and small fruits.

Asian Fairy-bluebird
Irena puella 24–27cm
Found in lowland and lower montane areas. Glossy, lacquer blue upperparts, and black underparts and flight feathers. Eyes red. If seen in low-light conditions, appears blackish in colour. Diet includes fruits, nectar and some insects. Can be seen in Gunung Raya area.

Orange-bellied Flowerpecker
Dicaeum trigonostigma 7–9cm

A fairly colourful garden bird that is fast and active. Male is bright greyish blue with yellow or orange underparts and small orange splotch on back; female is quite dull. Active throughout the mornings and found where flowers are blooming around commercial areas, resort grounds and forest edges. Feeds on small fruits, plus insects and nectar.

White-headed Munia
Lonchura maja 9–11cm

Small bird with pale brown plumage and white on entire head and throat, sometimes pale pinkish. One of the most popular of the four main species of munia found here. Feeds on rice and grass seeds, and very active during the rice-harvest season. Seen in flocks at *padi* fields around Langkawi; otherwise at wetland areas where tall grass or reeds are found.

Eurasian Tree Sparrow
Passer montanus 12.5–14cm

Commonly spotted around the island in both urban areas and near wetland habitats. A close relative of the common House Sparrow, they are smaller with a wingspan of about 21cm and an average weight of 24g. Rufous cap, black and white cheek, and small area of black on throat. They feed on seeds.

Grey Wagtail
Motacilla cinerea 18–19cm

Perhaps one of the hardest birds to see in lowland to montane forests, but not rare. Favours fast-flowing mountain streams and rivers, and occasionally seen on roads or trails leading up hills or mountains. Very long, black-and-white tail, yellow rump and yellow belly. Grey above with black wings. Wagging tail is its most obvious feature. Diet includes adult flies, mayflies, ants, beetles, crustaceans and molluscs.

Common Myna
Acridotheres tristis 25cm

These are the most common birds to see all over Langkawi and are easily identified by their brown body and black hooded head with bare yellow patch behind the eye. Bill and legs are bright yellow. Base of primaries, and all upper and lower coverts are white. Sexes are similar and birds are usually seen in pairs where the male seems larger. Often a nuisance and adapts well in urban areas.

Asian Glossy Starling
Aplonis panayensis 17–20cm

Very common, noisy bird sighted all over the island, often at resort grounds. At one glance it looks black, but plumage is black with greenish gloss overall, except on vent, which is matt black, and eyes are red. Juvenile has dark brown upperparts with weak green gloss on upper wings, and streaked breast. Feeds on fruits, including berries, nuts, and nectar from fruiting trees. Often seen in flocks almost anywhere around Langkawi.

Turtles

Malayan Soft-shell Turtle
Dogania subplana 30–35cm
(Forest Soft-shell Turtle)

Colour medium to dark brownish-green. Well camouflaged in water. Upper surface bears longitudinal stripes and underside orange. Head relatively large and nose tubular in shape. Usually found in clear, fast-flowing streams and quiet, muddy backwaters. Feeds on snails and other molluscs.

Asian Box Turtle
Cuora amboinensis 15–20cm
(Amboina Box Turtle, Southeast Asian Box Turtle, Malayan Box Turtle)

Blackish-brown to olive-brown shell, and blackish-olive head with three yellow stripes on sides. Not easily spotted but can be seen in lowland tropical forests near streams, ponds, *padi* fields and wet areas. Feeds on waxworms, fish, crickets and many other types of insect, plus aquatic plants and some fruits. Often reared as pets by locals.

Green Sea Turtle
Chelonia mydas 1–1.5m

One of the largest sea turtles found around Langkawi, and most easily seen while snorkelling or scuba diving. Migratory species that can swim more than 2,600km to reach its spawning grounds. Young blackish-brown with overall white lining. Adults entirely brown spotted or marbled with variegated rays. Prefers tropical waters and seen around Pulau Payar Marine Park and other smaller islands. Sometimes on secluded beaches, where it lays eggs. Listed as Endangered on IUCN Red List.

Lizards

Common Butterfly Lizard
Leiolepis belliana 15–40cm

One of the most easily seen lizards on the island, and often at resort grounds where short grass grows. Differs from the Malayan Butterfly Lizard due to its distinctive black-orange markings and underbelly colour. Approachable by humans up to a few metres, running to burrow when alarmed. Found in open areas such as disturbed agricultural land, sandy coastal habitats and golf courses.

Asian Gliding Lizard
Draco maculatus 8–9cm

Possesses good camouflage. Body ground colour varies from pale grey to brownish, often blending with tree trunks. Easily identified by yellow gular flag and blue spot at base. Often seen in secondary forests, rubber plantations and forest-edge locations with high levels of sunshine. Feeds mainly on ants.

Gunung Raya Green-crested Lizard
Bronchocela rayaensis 8–11cm

Beautiful green lizard. Head squarish. Top overall fully green, underpart yellowish green. Back of neck has small row of spikes and eye is black and green with a unique orange iris. Found in the rainforest areas usually climbing tree trunks or branches. They eat cicadas and many other small insects.

Many-lined Sun Skink
Mabuya multifasciata 33–35cm
Langkawi has a total of nine skink species. This one is easily identified by whitish-yellow throat, scaly skin and small, olive-brown to reddish-orange legs. Five or seven dark lines on ventral surface parallel to body line. Found in lowland rainforests along forest trails or tree trunks near riverbanks, mangroves and streams. Often seen slithering among the undergrowth in leaf litter and vegetation.

Speckled Forest Skink
Mabuya macularia 15–18cm
(Bronze Mabuya, Bronze Grass Skink)
One of Langkawi's most distinctive skinks due to its beautiful iridescent body scales. Body mainly brown to grey with dark stripe on each side bordered with white or cream. Frequents open forest, usually foraging or basking in low vegetation. Also found in plantations and abandoned areas.

Mangrove Skink
Emoia atrocrostata 24–26cm
Semi-aquatic skink found primarily in mangroves, back-beach vegetation and rocky shorelines. Grey or brownish-grey, flecked with black. Faint black band along each side. Throat bluish, and belly greenish or (usually) yellowish-orange. Feeds on insects and other invertebrates during low tide.

Spiny-tailed House Gecko
Hemidactylus frenatus 11–13.5cm
(Common House Gecko)
Easily seen all over Langkawi, including
in urban areas in homes and even offices.
Territorial. In the wild, seen in forest-
edge settings, including highly disturbed
habitats and mangroves. Identified by
various shades of brown or grey with
darker speckles, and short spines around
tail part. Seen on walls near lighting
fixtures, where it feeds mainly on flying
insects.

Tokay Gecko
Gekko gecko 28–30cm
One of the sought-after geckos by
poachers. In native habitats such as
rainforests, lives on trees and cliffs. This
large territorial gecko's skin is soft to the
touch. Generally grey with red speckles,
and able to change colour of skin to blend
into the environment. Has adapted to
rural human habitations, roaming walls
and ceilings at night in search of insect
prey.

Langkawi Island Bent-toed Gecko
Cyrtodactylus langkawiensis 20–23cm
Endemic to Langkawi. Body colour brown
or greyish-brown. Four or five dark bands
edged with pale scales extend across body.
Has 11–16 dark bands on tail. Restricted
to karst habitats dominated by limestone
rocks, and sandstone habitats. Preference
for rock crevices near the forest floor.
Seen in Datai Bay area.

Mahsuri's Rock Gecko
Cnemaspis mahsuriae 4cm
Recently discovered on Gunung Raya. This tiny species has slender, clawed digits which are cylindrical at the base; the distal phalanges are compressed, the lower surface has a row of plates. Body is depressed and granular looking. Tail is not compressed. Pupils are circular; eyelid distinct around the eye. Males have a pre-anal pore.

Common Water Monitor
Varanus salvator 1.5–2m
(Asian Water Monitor, Malayan Water Monitor, Biawak *Air*)
Largest lizard found in Langkawi, and native to Asia. Body colour dark brown or blackish. Yellow spots on underside. Very long neck and elongated snout. Excellent swimmer and known to climb trees, and to defend itself using its tail, claws and jaws. Diet includes fish, frogs, rodents, birds, crabs and snakes.

Clouded Monitor
Varanus nebulosus 1–1.7m
(Southeast Asian Monitor)
Medium-sized with slender body. Colouration comprises yellow spots on brown-grey base. Terrestrial species found in habitats as diverse as scrubland, rainforest and areas around villages. Excellent tree climber and digs among leaf litter searching for beetles and other insects.

Snakes

Paradise Flying Snake
Chrysopelea paradisi 1–1.2m
(Paradise Tree Snake)

Mostly found in moist rainforests. Can fly or glide a horizontal distance of about 100m from top of a tree. Body has overall black 'netting' pattern on golden yellow or green, sometimes with row of red flowery patterning along centre. Hunts small prey, mainly tree-dwelling lizards. Seen in coastal, lowland and secondary forests, and sometimes in parks and gardens.

Malayan Pit-viper
Calloselasma rhodostoma 76–91cm

Not endemic though called 'Malayan'. Colour reddish, greyish or pale brown, with two series of large, dark brown, black-edged triangular blotches that are alternating or opposite. The only Asian pit-viper with large crown scales and smooth dorsal scales. Seen in coastal forests, bamboo thickets, unused and overgrown farmland, orchards, plantations and forests around plantations, where it searches for rats and mice.

Mangrove Snake
Boiga dendrophila 2–2.5m
(Yellow-ringed Cat Snake)

Commonly found in mangrove areas of Langkawi, and endemic to Southeast Asia. Nocturnal hunter often lying motionless on branches by day. Colour black with yellow transverse bands. Feeds on rodents, small birds and their eggs, frogs, bats and sometimes other snakes. Easily seen during mangrove tours but visitors should avoid getting too close as the species is mildly venomous.

Mangrove Viper
Trimeresurus purpureomaculatus
66–100cm
(Mangrove Pit-viper, Shore Pit-viper)
One of the more venomous snakes in Langkawi, often spotted in mangroves. Colour varies from olive and greyish, to dark purplish-brown; whitish, greenish or brown below, uniform or spotted with brown. Seen in mangroves and coastal forests, and should not to be approached. Rests on branches by day and active at night.

Reticulated Python
Malayopython reticulatus 7–10m
Documented as the longest snake in the world. Identified by zigzag arrangement of black lines interspersed with yellow-brown and dark brown or medium-grey patches, with white spots. Feeds on small deer and wild pigs, constricting and suffocating prey before ingesting it. May eat rats, cats and chickens. Found from lowland to lower montane forests, agricultural areas, scrubland, mangrove edges, and sometimes villages and towns.

Monocellate Cobra
Naja kaouthia 1.5–2.3m
Not easy to see. Identified by circular marking on back of hood. Dorsal scales along back can range from yellow or grey to brown and even black. Terrestrial and most active at dusk. When threatened raises anterior portions of body, spreads hood, hisses loudly and strikes in an attempt to bite and defend itself. Found in habitats associated with water, such as *padi* fields, swamps and mangroves; also grassland, shrubland and forests. Feeds on small mammals, snakes and fish. Highly venomous.

Frogs

Answering Froglet
Microhyla heymonsi 1.6–2.6cm
(Dark-sided Chorus Frog)
Small and not that easy to see, but its
call is probably the most common (and
loudest) frog call heard in rainforests.
Small head with black stripe running along
sides of body. Back yellowish-brown with
thin white stripe along vertebrae, and
underside white. Found in temporary rain
puddles, *padi* fields, ditches, marshes and
slow-flowing streams.

Rice Field Frog
Limnocharis (fejervarya) 5–6cm
(Boie's Wart Frog, Asian Grass Frog)
Brownish with darker blotches,
sometimes with greenish or reddish
suffusion or tinge. Long toes on hind legs
and white belly. Commonly found in *padi*
fields, forest clearings, parks, gardens and
oil-palm plantations.

Mangrove Frog
Rana cancrivora 8–10.7cm
(Crab-eating Frog)
Mangrove dweller that can tolerate both
marine and fresh water conditions. Eyes
relatively large with blotches of pale
brown and dark brown as body colour.
Found mostly in mangrove wetlands,
marshes and sometimes *padi* fields.

Mudskippers

Dusky-gilled Mudskipper
Periophthalmus variabilis 5–6.5cm

Commonly seen in mangroves, this mudskipper is much smaller than others. Dorsal surface mottled light and dark brown, with vague dark brown saddles. Tail-fin mottled brown, and reddish-orange at margin. Seen at low tide, often in colonies. Shy when approached.

Boddart's Blue-spotted Mudskipper
Boleophthalmus boddarti 10–14cm

One of the most beautiful mudskippers. Easily recognized by blue spots on flank and cheeks. Dark bands on flanks, and large, bulging eyes. Highly territorial. Diet includes plant material as well as small invertebrates. Often seen at low tide along mangroves.

Crustaceans

Horseshoe Crab
Tachypleus gigas 34–42cm
(*Belangkas*)

Known as a living fossil, horseshoe crabs have unique shells that can be spotted in the sea or on beaches. They are similar to trilobites. Colour greenish-brown, and long, spiny tail, known as a telson. Blood is bright blue and medically important for its antibacterial properties. Usually seen on sandy and muddy shores or at depths to 40m (130ft). Diet includes worms, molluscs and sometimes seaweed.

Horn-eye Ghost Crab
Ocypode ceratophthalmus 6–8cm

Common medium-sized crab but not easy to see and usually active at night. Moves very fast over sand, hence the name 'ghost'. Squarish, box-like body bluish-grey, with brown markings on back and darker markings towards rear in shape of an 'H'. Roams beaches during low tide and easily scared. Scavenger, eating dead animals on shore, from fireworms to fish, shrimps and other crabs.

Strawberry Hermit Crab
Coenobita perlatus 6–8cm

Relatively hard to see. Body reddish-brown and orange, covered with white granules. Land hermit crabs are decapods, which means that they have ten legs (five pairs); when they no longer fit their shells they look for bigger ones. Found in coastal shorelines, tidal pools, sandy areas and humid locations with dune vegetation. Scavenger, eating a variety of dead and rotting material found along seashores.

Fiddler crabs
Uca spp. 2–4cm

Easily recognized by distinctively asymmetric claws. Communicates by sequence of waves and gestures. Male uses major claw to perform waving display as form of female courtship. Male versus male competition often occurs. If a male loses his larger claw, the smaller one will begin to grow larger and the lost claw will regenerate into a new smaller claw. Seen along mangrove banks and salt marshes in Langkawi, and occurs in various colours.

Spiders

Long-horned Orb-weaver
Macracantha arcuata 1.5–2.6cm
Female possesses pair of very long, curved spines on abdomen. Often brightly coloured in red, yellow and orange. Builds spiral, wheel-shaped web about 1–1.2m in size. Seen in lowland primary forests around the island and also in Datai Bay area.

Giant Golden Orb-weaver
Nephila pilipes 15–20cm
One of the largest orb-weaving spiders in the world. Web vertical with fine, irregular mesh, and not symmetrical, with hub usually nearer top. Male 4–10 times smaller than female. Legs black, and body with black, yellow and orange colouring. Seen in lowland rainforests around Langkawi, often busy spinning web. Diet includes insects like cicadas and flies, and occasionally small birds and bats.

Adanson's House Jumping Spider
Hasarius adansoni 6–8mm
(Adanson's House Jumper)
Male mostly black, with red 'mask' and two big white spots in rear part of upper surface of abdomen, and sometimes smaller pair of white dots even closer to spinnerets. Female dark brown. Seen in and around human habitation, on walls of homes and offices, and in parks and gardens. Hunts by leaping swiftly on unsuspecting prey, often from several centimetres away.

Butterflies

Red Helen Swallowtail
Papilio helenus 8–11.5cm

One of the sought-after butterflies in Langkawi. Large swallowtail seen in rainforests. Colour overall brownish-black, with white or grey-white scales and purple-red circlets towards bottom. Seen in midland rainforests towards higher elevations in Langkawi. Notable places include Gunung Raya and Darulaman Sanctuary.

Green Banded Peacock
Papilio palinurus 8–10cm

One of the beautiful butterflies seen in Langkawi. Dorsal sides of wings covered by powder of green scales, and background varies from dark greenish to black, with broad, bright emerald-green metallic bands. Seen at Darulaman Sanctuary, Datai Bay area, and rarely found elsewhere. Fast and restless flight.

Malayan Birdwing
Troides amphrysus 15–18cm

Large butterfly. In male uppersides of forewings black or dark brown, with veins bordered by pale to bright yellow. Female's basic colour black or dark brown, with veins bordered by white. High flier at 20–30m in rainforest canopy. Found in primary and secondary rainforests around Langkawi, and best spotted from early to late morning.

Golden Birdwing
Troides aeacus 15–16 cm

Large butterfly. Male's forewings black with veins bordered by whitish colour; hindwings bright yellow. Female larger than male, with dark brown or black wings. When flying it looks like a bird, hence the name 'birdwing'. Seen at Darulaman Sanctuary and found in primary and secondary rainforests at up to 800m.

Yellow Glassy Tiger
Parantica aspasia 6–7.5cm

One of the sought-after butterflies in Langkawi. Bluish-grey wings, with bright yellow and rather large basal patch and black markings. When resting, hangs upside down on dried branches, usually with wings folded shut. Found in forested areas in Langkawi, at Darulaman Sanctuary and around Datai Bay. Flies slowly and often glides in mid-air.

Striped Blue Crow
Euploea mulciber 8–9cm

Male dark brown entirely glossed with bright blue in forewing. Female lighter brown with forewing only glossed with blue on disc. Easily seen at Darulaman Sanctuary and in mangrove habitats and wasteland; sighted around urban parks, gardens and resort grounds in Langkawi.

Cycad Blue
Chilades pandava pandava 2.5–3cm
These butterflies have pale brown wings, with a metallic blue or purple sheen. They have eye patterns of orange and black on margin of hindwings, and each has a little tail attached. They lay pale white-blue, disk-shaped eggs on young, soft leaves of cycads. Caterpillars are green when they hatch, but become dark brown/deep burgundy as they grow older.

Great Orange Tip
Hebomoia glaucippe 8–10 cm
White with bright orange and black forewing tips. Underside is similar, but hindwings are light brown and resemble the surface of a dead leaf. Males and females look similar. Males spend most of their time perching on the ground with their wings closed. In this position they look like a dead leaf and are camouflaged from predators.

Dragonflies and Damselflies

Red Glider
Tramea transmarina 4.2–4.5cm
(Northern Glider, Saddlebag Glider)
Adult male has dark brown thorax, translucent hindwings and bright red abdomen, making it easy to identify. Eyes dark brown on top and greyish-white below. Female similar but duller. Often seen near small streams or wet areas gliding into the wind 5–10m above the ground. When perching, prefers to do so on emergent vegetation.

Blue Marsh Hawk
Orthetrum glaucum 3.8–4cm
(Asian Skimmer, Common Blue Skimmer)

Medium-sized dragonfly with dark face and greenish-blue eyes. Thorax dark blue due to pruinescence. Wings transparent with dark amber-yellow tint in extreme base. Female has yellowish-orange thorax. River and stream dweller often seen resting on twigs or rocks. Found in lowland rainforests and urban areas.

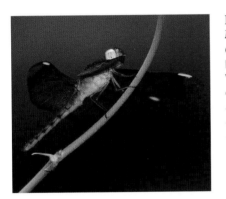

Red Grasshawk
Neurothemis fluctuans 3–3.4cm

Quite a commonly seen dragonfly. Male has brownish-red thorax and abdomen. Wings almost entirely brownish-red except for tips and thin, tapering clear band around hind margin. Female light brown and greyish when old, with dark streaks along abdomen and clear wings. Not particularly shy and often seen around very small streams, marshes and water areas in rainforests, as well as in commercial areas, for example in grassy drains.

Rufous Marsh Glider
Rhodothemis rufa 4–4.4cm
(Common Redbolt, Spine-legged Redbolt)

Common dragonfly with red eyes, thorax and abdomen, and clear wings. Female brown with yellow stripe at top of mid-dorsal area. Seen in commercial areas, marshes, open ponds and small ponds. Usually sighted perched on small leaves with wings open.

Greater Bluewing
Rhyothemis plutonia 2.8–3cm
One of the most beautiful dragonflies in Langkawi. Male and female alike and very colourful, with bluish-green metallic colour with hints of yellow and magenta. Thorax deep blue to black. Seen at lakes, ponds and irrigation channels in *padi* fields.

Rainforest Elf
Tetrathemis irregularis 2.5–3cm
Relatively small dragonfly. Black and yellow, large bluish-green eyes and transparent wings. Male and female similar and species is not easy to spot. Usually seen near rivers, swamps or ponds, in or close to lowland rainforests. Perches on vegetation or twigs close to the water's edge.

Orange-tailed Marsh Dart
Ceriagrion cerinorubellum 3.1–3.5cm
Common medium-sized damselfly with overall yellowish-green thorax, greenish-blue eyes, and brick-red colours on thorax and end of abdomen. Wings transparent. Female similar to male but may be a little duller in colour. Seen in weedy lakes, ponds and marshes, mostly in primary and secondary rainforest areas.

Beetles

Golden-spotted Tiger Beetle
Cicindela aurulenta 1.6–1.8cm
Colourful beetle. Dark blue-green, with six large yellow or bluish spots, and two smaller spots on shoulders. Legs spiny with fluorescent green tips. Found in a wide range of sandy habitats, including near shorelines, river bars, sand dunes, mangrove fragments and forest trails. Eats just about anything it can catch, which is usually other invertebrates.

Asiatic Rhinoceros Beetle
Oryctes rhinoceros 3–5cm
(Coconut Rhinoceros Beetle)
Major pest in coconut and oil-palm plantations. Usually black or very dark brown in colour. Possesses horn used for leverage when moving within tightly packed leaves. Found mostly where palms grow in coastal and lowland forests, and in urban areas. Chews big holes in palm leaves, then feeds on soft tissue in the heart of the palm.

Mangrove Jewel Bug
Calliphara nobilis 1–1.5cm
(Metallic Shield Bug)
Can only be seen in mangroves around Langkawi. Wide range of iridescent metallic hues that change with the view angle. Colours often change or become duller when the beetles are dried. Lives in mangroves all around Langkawi and often under mangrove leaves, frequently feeding on developing seeds.

Plants

Spotted Mangrove
Rhizophora stylosa 12–15m
(Red Mangrove, Stilt-rooted Mangrove)

Common mangrove plant with dark brown
to black, single or multiple trunks. Eye-
shaped leaves, and fruits brown in colour,
upside-down pear shaped, and about 4cm
long. Grows in muddy, sandy and stony
soil, as well as in corals along wetlands.

Mangrove Apple
Sonneratia alba 30–40m
(Firefly Mangrove)

One of the larger mangrove trees, with
beautiful pom-pom, white, pleated flowers
that bloom from dusk to dawn. These are
pollinated by local bats. Leaves obovate
shape and rounded. Also referred to as
the Firefly Mangrove due to the insects
that gather around it at night. Found at
seaward sides of mangroves, and usually a
very large tree. Popular place to see it is at
Kubang Badak BioGeoTrail.

Grey Mangrove
Avicennia marina 8–14m
(White Mangrove)

Popular tree in intertidal zones of
estuarine areas. Bark light grey. Leaves
glossy green on upper surface and silvery-
white on bottom. Flowers borne in white
to golden-yellow clusters and no larger
than 1cm. Seen around Kilim Geoforest
Park, Kubang Badak BioGeoTrail and
other mangrove areas in Langkawi.

Bungor Langkawi
Lagerstroemia Langkawiensis 6–30m
(Rose of India)

Endemic to Langkawi. Small to medium tree with oblong leaves that are red in colour when young and turn green when mature. Flowers pink with 5–6 petals each. Fruit is a capsule with elliptic-oblong shape. Usually found in open lowland rainforest areas in Langkawi.

Cliff Cycad
Cycas clivicola 5–8m
(Mountain Sago)

One of the rare plants in Langkawi due to the fact that it grows on limestone cliffs. Trunk dark grey and leaves green. The ancient palm-like cycads, whose lineage dates back 220 million years, predate all other plants except ferns. Grows at Kilim Geoforest Park. Can easily be seen with the naked eye and often grows solitarily.

Double-blooming Coral Hibiscus
Hibiscus rosa-sinensis 1.5–2m
(Bunga raya)
(Common Redbolt, Spine-legged Redbolt)

This species was introduced to Malaysia in the twelfth century. The Double-blooming Coral Hibiscus is one of many hybrid hibiscuses in Malaysia. Usually a bushy tree with trumpet-shaped, five-petal flowers; hybrids have double petals with one pistil, stamens and stigma. Grows easily due to the perfect tropical climate. Cultivated at some resort landscaped areas, one notable place being Langkawi Lagoon.

Sea Hibiscus
Hibiscus tiliaceus 4–10m
(Beach Hibiscus, Coastal Cottonwood, Bebaru)

Flowering tree in the mallow family; trunk 15cm in diameter. Branches curve over time. Flowers are bright yellow with a deep red centre upon opening. During the day flowers deepen to orange and finally red before they fall. Leaves are heart-shaped; undersides are covered in downy hairs, known technically as trichomes.

Tiger Orchid
Grammatophyllum speciosum 1.5–2m
(Sugar Cane Orchid, Queen of the Orchids, Giant Orchid)

Not an easy orchid to see and rare in the wild, but Tiger Orchids are found in Langkawi. Flowers yellow with maroon spots, and 10cm in diameter. They bloom at 4–5 years. Grows in the wild in tropical lowland forestsi. Can easily be seen at the Langkawi Orchid Farm

Blue Twilight
Pseuderanthemum andersonii 0.5–1m
(Florida Twilight, Blue Crossandra)

One of the beautiful flowering plants that bloom in the early part of the year, in January–March. Introduced ornamental species that grows in the wild in Langkawi. Flower colour more lilac than blue, and flower about 1.5cm in size. Easily seen at Darulaman Sanctuary in Lubuk Semilang, and also in other lowland rainforest areas of Langkawi.

PART 4: TRAVEL MATTERS

Practicalities

Unlike in much of Malaysia, the weekend in Langkawi is observed on Friday and Saturday, with Sunday being a working day. However, this really does not affect holidaymakers, as many shops, restaurants and bars remain open on all days.

Entry Requirements

Visas may be required by a small number of nationalities; it is advisable to check with the respective countries before departure. Passports require six months' validity and at least two blank pages. They need to be carried at all times for proof of identity, and spare passport photos are always useful.

Immigration and customs officers at Langkawi International Airport process all incoming international flights but not domestic ones. Langkawi is a duty-free port and customs officers mostly take a liberal approach to the amount of goods departing passengers are carrying, but it best to know the limits and adhere to them. Similar procedures operate for those travelling to and from Thailand. International visitors entering Malaysia for the first time via Langkawi need not complete any paperwork. However, biometric data is gathered and an immigration officer takes a photograph and records fingerprints.

Health

Langkawi is just north of the Equator and numerous tropical diseases are prevalent

Enjoy duty free shopping at Langkawi International Airport

although the situation is perhaps not as bad as many people may think. Precautions against malaria and dengue fever should be taken, and medical advice sought in the event of contagion, as both are complex diseases.

Both diseases are spread by mosquitos so avoiding them is the best solution. However, on tropical islands like Langkawi, this is easier said than done as cases of dengue fever especially have risen dramatically around the globe in the past few decades. Spread by the *Aedes mosquito*, the highest number of cases of dengue fever in Malaysia was 120,836 in 2015, with 336 deaths. Figures for subsequent years have not abated. Known as 'break-bone fever', symptoms include headaches, high fever, joint and muscle pain, extended periods of lethargy, and hot and cold flushes. Fortunately, it is not contagious between people.

Visitors to Langkawi should not be alarmed if they occasionally see what looks like a thick fog emerging from between buildings at dusk or dawn. This is known as fogging, and involves specialized teams treating areas with a mist of insecticide that kills mosquitos. Prevention is, however, better than the cure. Mosquitos are most active at dawn and dusk, so it is recommended that those particularly susceptible to attack remain indoors at these times. Wearing loose, light clothing is advisable, as is using insect repellent.

Travelling with a small personal first-aid kit with basic medical supplies is also advisable. Plasters, cotton wool, gauze, thermometer, tweezers, sterile swabs, scissors, sterile rubber gloves, antiseptic cream and basic painkillers are all good supplies for a first-aid kit.

While there is a hospital and doctors' clinics on Langkawi, travellers are advised to take out travel insurance before going to Malaysia.

Money

There are ATMs, moneychangers and banks in the main tourist areas and airport in Langkawi. The currency is the Malaysian ringgit and is the only pricing used in all shops. Banking hours are Sunday–Thursday, 9.15 a.m. to 4.30 p.m. Credit cards are accepted by most businesses, restaurants and hotels.

Business and Shopping Hours

Most businesses open Sunday–Thursday, 9.00 a.m. to 5.00 p.m. Shopping centres in Kuah and tourist areas such as Pantai Cenang and Pantai Tengah are open from 10.00 a.m. to 10.00 p.m.

Staying in Touch

These days, nearly everyone is connected to the world via a smartphone or the internet. Local SIM cards are available on arrival at major airports, and the internet is freely available in most hotels. Cable television with international news is also available. Electricity in Langkawi is powered by 220-240 V.

Tourist Assistance

Before travelling, research your embassy or consulate address details in case you need to contact them while in Malaysia. Bear in mind that most are located in Kuala Lumpur, some distance from Langkawi. The same can be said for toll-free numbers for any travel insurance taken out. Tourist police are on hand in Malaysia to assist.

Tourist Offices Overseas

Tourism Malaysia has overseas offices in various locations, including:
Frankfurt, Germany (+49 69 4609-23420)
London, United Kingdom
(+44 20 7930-7932)
Los Angeles, USA (+1 21 3689-9702)
Singapore (+65 6532-6321)
Sydney, Australia (+61 2 9299-4441)
Paris, France (+33 1 4297-4171)
The Hague, the Netherlands
(+31 70 799-9173)
Vancouver, Canada (+16 4 689-8899)

Climate

Generally, the climate is hot and humid year round. The higher altitude location of Gunung Raya is a few degrees cooler than the lower area. Monsoon winds affect different parts of Langkawi at different times of the year. While there are regional differences, monsoon rains fall in November–April, with the dry season occurring in May–October.

During the day, moisture accumulates in the atmosphere, to be followed in the afternoon with a short, sharp rainfall, and days of lingering rain are rare. Most locals do not get too concerned when it rains and simply take shelter, knowing that the rain will soon clear. Motorcyclists may don wet-weather gear or seek shelter under an awning for the duration of a storm. Carrying a raincoat and/or umbrella makes good sense.

Religion, Holidays and Customs

Religion

Malaysians enjoy a harmonious atmosphere of religious tolerance and understanding, with Islam, Hinduism, Buddhism, Christianity and Taoism being the most common religions practised on the island.

The vast majority of Langkawi residents are Muslim and there are mosques all over the island. While visitors are welcomed at most, they are expected to wear conservative clothing and be mindful of people praying. It is best to avoid visiting mosques during prayers, which are conducted five times a day. It is always best to ask if in doubt and most islanders are happy to offer assistance.

Some Chinese shops, houses and even special locations may have an altar and shrine where joss sticks smoulder and fruit is offered. These should be left alone.

Most Indians in Langkawi are Hindus and there are several temples, mainly in the east and south-east. These include the colourful Kisap Temple (the oldest on the island) and the Sri Maha Mariamman Devasthanam to the south of Kisap. Visitors need to dress respectfully, remove their shoes at temple entrances and keep noise to a minimum. Hindus celebrate Deepavali (the date varies but it occurs sometime in October or November).

Christians celebrate church services in English, Tamil and Chinese at the Sanctuary of Glory near Langkawi Mall. Langkawi's Taoist devotees worship at the Thean Hou Temple on the outskirts of Kuah. Nearby are two Buddhist temples.

Festivals and Holidays

Langkawi has numerous public holidays, determined at either federal or state level. Some of the most important are described below.

Hari Raya Puasa falls at the end of the

Muslim fasting month of Ramadan, with the actual day determined by the sighting of the new moon by religious leaders. During Ramadan, Muslims abstain from eating and drinking from dawn until dusk. Things slow down during this time, but food and drinks are still available in non-Muslim operated restaurants. During the festivities that follow, houses are gaily lit and decorated. Many people open their houses for friends and visitors to drop by to snack.

Chinese New Year is celebrated in late January or early February to mark the beginning of the Chinese lunar year. Traditionally on this day, parents give children small amounts of money in an *ng pow* (red packet) as a symbol of luck and good health. The visiting of friends and family usually occurs on the first and second days of the festival.

Wesak Day (the day of the full moon in May), which marks the birth, enlightenment and death of Lord Buddha, is the most significant day in the Buddhist calendar. On this day, Buddhist temples are full of worshippers and priests.

Christmas Day marks the birth of Christ and is celebrated, with the festive spirit extending through December.

Customs and Etiquette

The people of Langkawi are welcoming but generally conservative in their lifestyle. Being a good guest is part of the travel experience, and knowledge of the various customs helps to avoid embarrassment. Different communities follow different customs, but here are a few generalizations to help smooth the path of travel.

Many locals remove their shoes before entering buildings, especially homes and places of worship; visitors are expected to do the same.

- Muslims use their right hand only when eating, and eating with the hand is not uncommon.
- Many women may not shake hands with men, so wait until a hand is offered.
- Many sections of mosques are not open to non-Muslims, and it is best to avoid mosques during prayers.
- While duty-free alcohol is freely available in resorts and tourist areas, it is not available in Muslim restaurants, villages or houses. Although some establishments remain open until late, rowdy and disorderly behaviour is frowned upon.
- Avoid placing the locals in a situation where they will lose face.
- Learn the important differences between *halal* and *haram*.
- Some locals are unhappy about being photographed and it is always polite to indicate your wishes before thrusting a camera into someone's face.
- The people of Langkawi are modest in their dress and expect visitors to show constraint – nude bathing is out, as is revealing clothing, and public displays of affection are also frowned upon. Respectable clothing is expected to be worn when visiting government offices.
- During the fasting month of Ramadan, the dates of which vary from year to year, Muslims fast from sunrise to sunset and it is respectful to avoid eating or drinking in front of them. Food and drinks may be difficult to obtain in parts of Langkawi during the day in many restaurants while Ramadan is observed.
- Using and importing drugs is a capital offence in Langkawi.

Food and Beverages

One of the joys of travel includes sampling exciting new dishes and enjoying local beverages. Langkawi does not disappoint in this respect, with many tantalizing tropical fruits, vegetables, spices and seafood being available. It is not only the food but also the places where it is purchased and consumed that make Langkawi fascinating to those who enjoy their food.

Malaysians live to eat so visitors to Langkawi are in for a smorgasbord of local and international cuisines served in venues ranging from simple local restaurants to fine-dining outlets in five-star resorts. Eating in the former offers excellent value for money, while the prices at the latter are comparable to those in resorts in similar destinations in the region.

Staples, Markets and Customs

Rice is the staple, and seafood, chicken and buffalo meat are the main sources of protein for most islanders. Rice is grown in *padi* fields on the flat lands of Langkawi.

Buying fresh produce has always

Lunchtime at a restaurant in Padang Matsirat

been and still is very important for most islanders, and night markets (*pasar malam*) are popular places to buy fruits, vegetables, locally caught fish and some meats. Night markets are held in different venues on different nights, with the most popular one being staged on Sunday evening from 5.00 p.m. to 8.00 p.m. at Padang Matsirat.

It is important for travellers to appreciate that Muslims eat and serve *halal* food, and that alcohol is not served in Muslim restaurants and in certain other venues. Many locals also eat food with their hand but only the right one. Visitors need to exercise constraint in consuming alcohol, especially in public areas frequented by Muslims. Many restaurants may close in daylight hours during the fasting month of Ramadan. However, at dusk stalls open to serve an array of dishes in a festive atmosphere.

Food styles in Langkawi follow the country's main racial groups of Malay, Chinese and Indian, although Indian food is not as well represented as it is in other parts of Peninsular Malaysia. Added to this are some tantalizing dishes from neighbouring Thailand.

Another complexity is that there is no one Chinese or Malay style, but rather a multitude of regional variations. In the case of Chinese food, the main regional styles are Cantonese, Hokkien, Hainanese Teochew, Szechuan and Hakka, which generally are mildly spiced.

Stalls and Snack Food

Snacking is common, with many people eating five small meals of breakfast, lunch, tea, dinner and supper. Short breaks are often taken in coffeeshops (*kedai kopi*) where *teh tarik* (local tea) is the preferred

everage, while others may order café
tte in a globally recognized outlet.

cclaimed Dishes

pices, chilli, garlic, coconut milk, onions,
emongrass, ginger and *sambal belacan*
spicy chilli and prawn condiment) are
mportant ingredients in many dishes
repared by Langkawi chefs. Fresh
eafood is caught in the waters of
angkawi and served in many restaurants.
he illumination on the water on the
orizon each evening is produced by the
umerous boats that fish here.

Some well-known local dishes include
ksa (spicy noodle soup, with the local
ariety being *Kedah laksa*), beef *rendang*
spicy beef), *mee goreng* (fried noodles),
an bakar (barbecued fish), *nasi campur*
ice smorgasbord), *kuih muih* (Malay
akes), *pisang goreng* (fried banana
ritters), *ayam percik* (grilled chicken
narinated in coconut milk and spices),
eef noodle soup, *kway teow* and *satay*
neat on skewers grilled over charcoal
ames).

Football-sized, spiky durians ('the king
f fruits'), coconuts and local cashew nuts
re grown on Langkawi. Mozzarella is
lso made on the island using local buffalo
nilk.

The people of Langkawi enjoy hawker
ood while visitors can seek out global
uisines, especially in the main tourist
reas. Japanese, Thai, Chinese, Indian,
.orean, German, Mexican, Middle
astern, French and Italian cuisines are
vailable. Fast food and international
offee/tea concepts complete the culinary
fferings.

There are numerous simple stalls
ll over the island, often serving one
peciality dish. Some places have

Spicy Langkawi laksa

more extensive listings – Siti Fatimah
Restaurant, located near the hospital,
serves 72 dishes in its *nasi campur* lunch.
Another notable and acclaimed venue
is Nam Restaurant in Bon Ton Resort. It
takes a 'West meets spice' approach to
the food served, with a speciality dish
being the 'Nyonya special' (eight dish
local platter plus dessert). The setting,
overlooking a lily-lined wetland, is perfect,
especially at sunset.

Dining Precincts

All the main tourist areas have places to
eat, with the main precincts being Pantai
Cenang, Pantai Tengah, Kuah, Fisherman's
Wharf at the Royal Langkawi Yacht Club,
Telaga Harbour and the food trucks along
the road on the northwestern border to
the airport runway.

Being a duty-free island, alcohol
prices are reasonable even in five-star
resorts. Sunsets along the western
side of the island in places like Pantai
Cenang and Pantai Tengah especially are
often spectacular, with numerous bars
capitalizing on their location and usually
employing happy hour prices.

Green Accommodation

Travellers are becoming more discerning in their accommodation choices, and many hoteliers are reducing the environmental impacts of their operations. Most international hotel operators on Langkawi follow corporate environmental guidelines with mixed enthusiasm, but the following properties are making strident efforts to make their operations environmentally friendly.

Bon Ton Resort

What was once a tranquil, coconut-lined beachfront morphed into a lily-lined wetland when the shallow coastal waters were reclaimed to accommodate the extension of the airport runway. Perched at the interface between the land and the reedy wetlands is Bon Ton Resort, a unique collection of eight antique Malay houses and a fine example of cultural preservation. These were relocated to their current site in a 100-year-old coconut plantation to offer guests memorable and luxurious interiors, as well as the opportunity to admire some local architecture. The wetlands in front of Bon Ton's Nam Restaurant are one of the best venues on the island for birdwatchers keen on sighting waterbirds, shorebirds and even hornbills among the coconut palms. As a courtesy, non-guests are expected to avail themselves of the restaurant/bar's services. Bon Ton also operates LASSie, a shelter for neglected, abused and needy animals. Guests can contribute to support these efforts. www.bontonresort.com

Blue House, Bon Ton Resort

Frangipani Langkawi Resort and Spa

Frangipani is internationally recognized for its green practices in several key areas – water conservation, energy conservation, farming management and waste management. The resort captures rainwater in numerous water tanks to use for cleaning, irrigation, toilet flushing and laundry. It has put in place energy-conservation measures, including solar panels and energy-saving bulbs.

Vegetables, herbs and fruit trees have been planted, with the produce consumed in the resort. Organic fertilizer from composting and vermiculture from garden waste provide soil nutrients. In addition to food crops, the resort raises chickens, ducks, geese and fish for aesthetic, educational and consumption purposes.

Guests' waste is sorted at source, making waste separation and recycling an easy and efficient task for staff. Much of the wastewater is treated via an effective natural biological system, then used for crop irrigation.

Courses are conducted by resort staff to train other hoteliers and interested parties in greening activities. www.frangipanilangkawi.com

Sunset Valley Holiday Homes

Sunset Valley is a collection of six wooden *kampung* (village-style) houses located in the centre of the island overlooking rice *padi* fields. All the houses were found on Langkawi, relocated and reconstructed.

Many trees have been planted here, including bamboo, which makes excellent windbreaks, and provides shade and protection for the local native wildlife. Various local fruit trees have been planted in the gardens (rambutan, cempedak, mangosteen, mango and petai), and lemon and kafir lime, plus plants such as lemongrass and flowering shrubs like hibiscus, frangipani and bougainvillea. The birdlife is prolific, with regular sightings of the Red-wattled Lapwing, Brahminy Kite, White-bellied Sea Eagle, Oriental Hornbill and Cattle Egret, as well as various orioles, drongos, woodpeckers, herons, kingfishers, bulbuls, sunbirds, munias and mynas. Dusky Leaf Monkeys, Crab-eating Macaques and Colugos are occasional visitors. The resort operates an active recycling and composting programme. www.sunsetvalleyholidayhouses.com

The Datai Langkawi

Located in the heart of the rainforest within Teluk Datai (rated one of the world's top ten beaches by *National Geographic*), the 121-room The Datai Langkawi has been highly regarded for its respect for nature since its opening in 1993. Blending into its surroundings and reusing trees felled during its construction, the architects and designers ensured minimum disruption to the site.

When an extensive refurbishment was started in 2017, sustainability and conservation initiatives were interwoven, including the creation of a long-term programme to sustain the bay's unique biodiversity and natural beauty, while providing more opportunities for engagement with the local community. Called the Datai Pledge, this was created by the resort's dedicated team of naturalists, marine biologists and sustainability personnel in partnership with local non-profit organizations. The programme has four aspects –resort operations, marine life, wildlife and the local youth.

An ambitious commitment to zero waste to landfill, consumption of less energy and water, and no single-use plastic is in place. To realize this, a bottling plant, permaculture garden, wastewater-management system and organic wealth centre, as well as recycling labs, have been created. The Nature Centre offers guided nature walks, mangrove kayak tours and talks. Dining outlets such as The Gulai House and The Pavilion enable guests to dine in natural settings and to admire displays of Colugos as they glide among the trees at sunset.

Nature also forms the base of the spa and well-being programmes, with specially crafted spa treatments and holistic activities.

In recognition of its initiatives, the resort has received accolades including the EarthCheck Silver Certification (EarthCheck is the world's leading environmental certification and benchmarking programme for the travel and tourism industry). The Datai Langkawi is the first organization in the world to be awarded the certification for terrestrial tourism projects. The Malaysian Ministry of Tourism, Arts and Culture has awarded the property with several Green Hotel awards. www.thedatai.com

Getting There and Travelling

Langkawi is well served by regular air and ferry services. Most travellers fly into Langkawi International Airport, while others use the ferry services from the mainland (Kuala Perlis and Kuala Kedah) and Penang Island or ports in southern Thailand (Satun and Koh Lipe). The closest train stations on the mainland are Arau and Alor Star, but passengers then need to travel by road and ferry to Langkawi.

By Air

Airlines based in Malaysia such as Malaysia Airlines, AirAsia, Firefly and Malindo operate scheduled flights into Langkawi from Kuala Lumpur (KLIA/KLIA2 and Subang), Penang and Johor Bahru. Charter flights from Europe occasionally operate to Langkawi during the European winter. Scoot has direct flights to and from Singapore, while Qatar Airways flies from Doha and China Southern connects to Guangzhou.

KLIA/KLIA2 is the international gateway for many overseas visitors. From here, passengers fly to Langkawi on a domestic airline. KLIA/KLIA2 are both about 60km (37 miles) or a one-hour drive from Kuala Lumpur's other airport, Sultan Abdul Aziz Shah in Subang (also known as Subang Skypark). For this reason, it does not make sense to transfer from KLIA/KLIA2 to Subang for a flight to Langkawi.

Subang is ideal for those staying in the western suburbs of Kuala Lumpur. Firefly and Malindo operate turboprop aircraft from here to Langkawi and other airports in Peninsular Malaysia, and there are international flights on Firefly to Singapore (Seletar Airport, not Changi), Banda Aceh (Indonesia) and Phuket (Thailand). The airport's facilities are good, and with fewer passengers, clearing immigration, customs and security is normally quicker than via KLIA/KLIA2. KTM train services link KL Sentral with Subang Skypark via the Skypark Link from Subang Jaya Station. Trains from KL Sentral depart from 5.30 a.m. to 9.25 p.m., and from the Skypark from 7.50 a.m. to 11.20 p.m. Passengers are then required to walk 300m (985ft) to the Skypark. However, many passengers use taxis or the park-and-fly car parks.

Flying time from Kuala Lumpur to Langkawi is approximately one hour, Penang about 30 minutes, and Singapore some 90 minutes.

Alor Star is another airport visitors can use to access Langkawi. Those who fly into what is the Kedah state capital then have a road and ferry journey to reach Langkawi.

The airport in Langkawi is located at Padang Matsirat. International travellers arriving directly from overseas complete immigration and customs procedures here. There are no air bridges – supposedly, having passengers walk down steps and across the tarmac was meant as an immediate introduction to Langkawi's tropical weather.

Facilities at the airport are good, with bags delivered from the plane via carousels. Eager car-rental agents greet passengers while they wait for their bags to be delivered. Other services and facilities include ATMs, moneychangers, baby-care room, Muslim prayer room, charging stations, Wi-Fi, duty-free shops, WHSmith, restaurants, airport lounges and Tourism Malaysia information counter.

By Sea

Ferries from Langkawi (the departure terminal is Kuah Jetty) connect to Kuala Perlis (in Perlis) and Kuala Kedah (in Kedah) as well as Satun (in southern Thailand) and Koh Lipe (Tarutao National Park in southern Thailand). Ferry capacities vary but most ferries from the mainland carry 100–450 passengers and those to Koh Lipe are smaller. There are more frequent ferry services during the Langkawi weekend (Friday and Saturday) and holidays, and the timings below should be used as guide (check ferry websites for more accurate departures). Ferry services during the fasting month of Ramadan are less frequent, but are usually more frequent during the Hari Raya holiday at the end of Ramadan.

The distance from Kuala Perlis to Langkawi is 31km (19 miles), and a ferry takes 75 minutes. Ferries to the island operate between 6.30 a.m. and 9.30 p.m. at 90-minute intervals. Ferries from Langkawi to Kuala Perlis operate from 7.30 a.m. to 9.00 p.m.

Kuala Kedah is 51km (32 miles) from Langkawi, with the journey taking 90 minutes. Ferries to Langkawi operate between 7.00 a.m. and 9.30 p.m. at 90-minute intervals. Those from Langkawi to Kuala Kedah depart between 7.00 a.m. and 9.00 p.m.

Penang is 110km (68 miles) to the south, and the ferry journey takes two hours 45 minutes. Daily ferries from Penang (Swettenham Pier) to Langkawi depart at 8.30 a.m. and 2.00 p.m., and from Langkawi to Penang at 10.30 a.m. and 3.00 p.m.

It is important to note that Thailand is one hour behind Malaysian time. There is normally a morning and afternoon ferry departure to and from Satun on the southern Thailand mainland. The journey of 42km (26 miles) takes 75 minutes.

During the peak season from October to May, there are regular ferry services from Telaga Harbour on Langkawi to Koh Lipe near Tarutao National Park in the Andaman Sea to the north-west of Langkawi. There is a morning and afternoon ferry to and from Langkawi to Koh Lipe. The distance is 42km (26 miles), and the journey takes about 90 minutes. As there is no jetty on Koh Lipe, passengers arrive directly on the beach. Like the journey to Satun, this is international travel, and all passengers are required to carry their passports. Due to the prevailing monsoon, there is no scheduled ferry service at other times of the year.

There were once big plans for cruise liners to regularly berth in Langkawi, but the well-equipped cruise terminal on the far south-east of the island in front of Resorts World Langkawi is only occasionally used.

By Train

While it is possible to travel to Kedah and Perlis by train (operated by Malaysia's Keratapi Tanah Melayu, or KTM), getting to Langkawi requires additional road and ferry connections. Adventurous travellers could use the train and alight at Arau Station in Perlis or Alor Star in Kedah, then travel by taxi or bus to the ports of Kuala Perlis or Kuala Kedah for a connecting ferry to Langkawi. While not the preferred connection for travellers coming from the south, train travellers arriving in Malaysia from Thailand could find this the most acceptable way to travel to Langkawi.

Those who use the train from Kuala Lumpur need to alight at Bukit Mertajam (near Butterworth and Penang), then catch a connecting train to Alor Star. From here, they must catch a bus or taxi to the port of Kuala Kedah, then a ferry across the Straits of Malacca to Langkawi. The total travelling time for those using this this route is about 10 hours.

By Road
Coach services operate from Kuala Lumpur to Kuala Kedah and Kuala Perlis, connecting to ferries for Langkawi. These trips take 6–8 hours. There is a roll-on, roll-off car ferry operating between Kuala Perlis and Langkawi for those who want to use their own car on Langkawi. Alternatively, park your car in the public car parks at both ports and take the ferry to Langkawi.

Exploring the Island
Rental cars, motorbikes and bicycles can all be hired on Langkawi. They offer an inexpensive way to explore the island, but it is always best to check your insurance cover in the event of an accident. Vehicles are normally hired with an empty tank.

Resources

Books

Bergbauer, M. & Kirschner, M. 2014. *Reef Fishes of the Indo-Pacific*. John Beaufoy Publishing.

Bowden, D. 2016. *Enchanting Borneo*. John Beaufoy Publishing.

Bowden, D. 2019. *Enchanting Penang*. John Beaufoy Publishing.

Bowden, D. 2020. *Enchanting Langkawi*. John Beaufoy Publishing.

Bowden, D. 2020. *Enchanting Malaysia*. John Beaufoy Publishing.

Das, I. 2021 2nd ed.. *A Naturalist's Guide to the Snakes of Southeast Asia*. John Beaufoy Publishing.

Davison, G. & Yeap Chin Aik. 2018. *A Naturalist's Guide to the Birds of Malaysia*. John Beaufoy Publishing.

Kirton, L. 2018. *A Naturalist's Guide to the Butterflies of Malaysia*. John Beaufoy Publishing.

Lim Kim Seng, Yong Ding Li & Lim Kim Chuah. 2019. *Field Guide to the Birds of Malaysia and Singapore*. John Beaufoy Publishing.

Saw Leng Guan. 2019. *A Naturalist's Guide to the Trees of Southeast Asia*. John Beaufoy Publishing.

Shepherd, C. R. & Shepherd, L. A. 2017. *A Naturalist's Guide to the Primates of Southeast Asia*. John Beaufoy Publishing.

Shepherd, C. R. & Shepherd, L. A. 2018. *A Naturalist's Guide to the Mammals of Southeast Asia*. John Beaufoy Publishing.

Yong Ding Li & Low Bing Wen. 2018. *The 125 Best Birdwatching Sites in Southeast Asia*. John Beaufoy Publishing.

Yusoff, I. *Birds of Lubuk Semilang, Langkawi, Malaysia*. e-book.

Websites

General

Bird Malaysia www.bird-malaysia.com
Bujang Valley Archaeological Museum www.jmm.gov.my
Global Geoparks Network www.globalgeopark.com
Keretapi Tanah Melayu (KTM) www.ktmb.com.my
LADA (Langkawi Development Authority) www.lada.gov.my; www.naturallylangkawi.com
Langkawi Geopark www.langkawigeopark.com.my
Malaysia Asia www.malaysia-asia.my
Malaysian Nature Society www.mns.my
MareCet (Marine Mammal Conservation) www.marecet.org
The Island Drum www.theislanddrum.com
Tourism Malaysia www.toursim.gov.my
UNESCO www.unesco.org
World Wide Fund for Nature www.wwf.org.my

Accommodation

Aloft Langkawi www.marriott.com/hotels/travel/lgkal-aloft-langkawi-pantai-tengah
Ambong Ambong Langkawi Rainforest Retreat www.ambong-ambong.com
Aseania Resort and Spa www.aseanialangkawiresort.com
Barkat Chalets www.agoda.com/barkat-chalets/hotel/langkawi-my
Bayview bhi.bayviewhotels.com
Bella Vista Waterfront splashoutlangkawi.com/home/bella-vista
Berjaya Langkawi Resort www.berjayahotel.com/langkawi
Bon Ton Resort bontonresort.com
Cabana Lipe www.cabanalipe.com
Casa Del Mar casadelmar-langkawi.com
Century Langkasuka Resort century-langkasuka-resort.h-rez.com
Dash Resort Langkawi www.dash-hotels.com/langkawi-malaysia
Eagle Bay www.eaglebay.com.my
Earth Lodge www.earthlodgemalaysia.com
Faridzuan Motel www.langkawipages.com/faridzuanmotel
Favehotel www.favehotels.com/en/hotel/view/16/favehotel-cenang-beach-langkawi
Federal Villa Beach Resort (via a booking site)
Four Seasons www.fourseasons.com/langkawi
Frangipani Langkawi Resort and Spa www.frangipanilangkawi.com
Holiday Villa www.holidayvillahotels.com/holiday-villa-beach-resort-spa-langkawi
Koh Lipe Castaway www.kohlipe.castaway-resorts.com
Langkawi Lagoon Sea Village www.langkawilagoon.com
Langkawi Seaview langkawiseaviewhotel.com
Langkawi Yacht Club Hotel langkawiyachtclubhotel.com
Mali Sunrise Beach www.maliresorts.com
MADA (Muda Agricultural Development Authority) www.mada.gov.my
ParkRoyal Langkawi Resort www.panpacific.com/en/hotels-and-resorts/pr-langkawi
Pelangi Beach Resort and Spa pelangiresort.com
Rebak Island Resort www.vivantahotels.com/en-in/vivanta-langkawi-rebak-island
Resort Noba www.facebook.com/Resortnobapulaulangkawi
Ritz Carlton Langkawi www.ritzcarlton.com/en/hotels/malaysia/langkawi
Serambi Boutique Resort Home (via booking sites)

Serendipity Beach www.serendipityresort-kohlipe.com
Smith House thesmith-house.com
St Regis Langkawi www.marriott.com/hotels/travel/lgkxr-the-st-regis-langkawi
Sunset Beach Resort www.langkawi-info.com/sunsetbeachresort
Sunset Valley Holiday Houses sunsetvalleyholidayhouses.com
Tanjung Rhu Resort tanjungrhu.com.my
Temple Tree www.templetree.com.my
The Andaman www.marriott.co.uk/luxury collection/langkawi
The Danna Langkawi www.thedanna.com
The Datai Langkawi www.thedatai.com
Tuba Beach Resort (via booking sites)
Wapi www.wapiresortkohlipe.com
Westin Langkawi www.marriott.co.uk/hotels/travel/lgkwi-the-westin-langkawi-resort-and-spa

Airlines and Ferries
AirAsia www.airasia.com
China Southern Airlines www.csair.com
Firefly www.fireflyz.com
Langkawi Ferry Line Ventures www.langkawiferryline.com
Langkawi Ferry Services www.langkawi-ferry.com
Malaysia Airlines www.malaysiaairlines.com
Malindo Air www.malindoair.com
Qatar Airways www.qatarairways.com
Scoot Airline www.flyscoot.com

Attractions
Atma Alam Batik Art Village www.atmaalam.com
Crocodile Adventureland Langkawi www.crocodileadventureland.com
Darulaman Sanctuary www.sanctuary.bdb.com.my
Galeria Perdana www.jmm.gov.my/en/museum/galeria-perdana

Laman Padi Langkawi/Rice Garden Museum m.facebook.com/lamanpadilangkawiofficial
Langkawi Canopy Adventure facebook.com/LCASB/
Langkawi Wildlife Park langkawiwildlifepark.com
Rebak Island Marina www.rebakmarina.com.
Resorts World Awana Marina www.rwlangkawi.com
RMSIR (Raja Muda Selangor International Regatta) www.rmsir.com
Royal Selangor Yacht Club www.rsy.com.my
Skycab panoramalangkawi.com/skycab
Skydive Langkawi skydivelangkawi.com
Skytrex Adventure Langkawi www.skytrex-adventure.org/langkawi
Splash Out Langkawi splashoutlangkawi.com
Telaga Harbour Marina www.telagaharbour.com
Umgawa Zipline Eco Adventures www.ziplinelangkawi.com
Underwater World Langkawi www.underwaterworldlangkawi.com

Travel Specialists
Malaysia
Asian Overland Services (+60 4 952-0000, ext. 8718, www.asianoverland.com.my).
The company operates a tour desk at Frangipani Resort Langkawi and can arrange island excursions plus other travel services throughout the whole of Malaysia.
Dev's Adventure Tours (+60 19 494-9193, www.langkawi-nature.com).
Well-established ecotourism operator in Langkawi with small group tours led

by passionate naturalists. Includes kayak tours, sea safaris, mangrove tours, cycling excursions, jungle treks and cooking classes. Uses glass-bottled water, and not plastic.

Australia

Malaysia is a popular destination for Australians, with Langkawi a much-visited holiday island. Intrepid Travel (www.intrepidtravel.com) offers tours that include Langkawi and Koh Lipe (Thailand). Wendy Wu Tours (www.wendywutours.com.au) offers various package tours to Malaysia, including trips to Langkawi. Peregrine Adventures (www.peregrineadventures.com.au) has various trips to Malaysia, including a small boat cruising adventure from Phuket (Thailand) to Penang with stops in Tarutao National Park (Thailand) and Langkawi.

United Kingdom

Abercrombie and Kent (www.abercrombiekent.co.uk) offers several tours of Malaysia, including overnight stops in Langkawi. Other outbound-tour operators include Exodus (www.exodus.co.uk), Explore (www.explore.co.uk) and Responsible Travel (www.responsibletravel.com).

Some Basic Bahasa Words and Phrases

thank you	terimah kasih
you're welcome	sama sama
my name is	nama saya
good morning	selamat pagi
good afternoon	selamat petang
good evening	selamat malam
where is … ?	dimana
how much is … ?	ini berapa
one	satu
two	dua
three	tiga
four	empat
five	lima
six	enam
seven	tujuh
eight	lapan
nine	sembilan
ten	sepuluh
100	se ratus
1,000	se ribu
bus station	stesen bus
taxi	teksi
beach	pantai
island	pulau
hill	bukit
mountain	gunung
river	sungai
town	bandar
water	air
eat	makan
drink	minum
expensive	mahal
cheap	murah
can	boleh
cannot	tak boleh
man	lelaki
women	perempuan
toilet	tandas

Nature Escapes on the Mainland

Ulu Muda, Kedah

The 163,000ha (40,278 acres) greater Ulu Muda forest landscape is a collection of several forest reserves gazetted under the National Forestry Act. This large, contiguous forest complex, located in Kedah and bordering the Thai border, is an off-the-beaten-path destination that people staying on Langkawi may want to visit. Well known for its rich biodiversity, it is also an important catchment forest providing water to three constructed lakes – Ahning, Pedu and Muda. These in turn supply irrigation water for the vast *padi* growing region of the Kedah and southern Perlis plains. The area produces nearly 50 per cent of Malaysia's rice output, making Ulu Muda critically important for Malaysia's food security.

It is, however, the rich biodiversity of Ulu Muda that is attracting more and more researchers, naturalists and ecotourists. Dubbed the best place in Malaysia to see the Asian Elephant in the wild (recent sightings noted 29 in one herd), it is also home to all three large cats (Malayan

Spot wild elephants

Tiger, Leopard and Clouded Leopard) and most of the smaller cats. Additionally found here are the Malayan Tapir, Gaur (or Seladang), Honey Bear, Hairy-nosed Otter, Agile Gibbon and Serow.

The avifauna in Ulu Muda is also impressive, with a current bird list of 325 species. The count is ongoing, partly due to the fact that few birders previously spent time here. All ten species of Malaysian hornbill are found here (one of only two sites in Malaysia where this is the case), including the rare Plain-pouched Hornbill (best seen in June–September). Evening counts of several hundred are common, with the record being 1,720 individuals counted in one evening alone. Other birds of interest are the Malayan Honeyguide, Chestnut-necklace Partridge, White-fronted Scops-owl and Masked Finfoot.

The vast forest is still a very well-kept secret, and it seems that some want to keep it that way by only accommodating a limited numbers of guests at any one time. This is made easier because of the difficulty of access. Visitors do need to keep their expectations in check, however, because although the fauna list is impressive, this is a rainforest so sightings are difficult (rainforests are dark and thick, and can easily hide their wild denizens from prying eyes).

Forest reserves like Ulu Muda are easily degazetted and may be exploited for their timber. Efforts are presently ongoing to upgrade the area's protection to either a State or National Park. Gazettement will afford the area stronger protection to conserve biodiversity and the forest's function as a vital water-catchment resource.

Places to Stay

There are only two good accommodation options around Lake Muda. Earth Lodge, in the middle of the Ulu Muda rainforest, is highly recommended. To get there, guests have to take a one-hour boat ride on a *sampan* (traditional wooden boat) across Lake Muda and up the Muda River. Depending on the water level, it can take a little longer to get to the lodge. Because of its remote location, the lodge only accepts advance bookings. Being off grid, it generates its own electricity and treats its own river water.

The lodge does not offer daily room rates but rather three-, four- or five-day packages for dorms and rooms. All include boat transfer from and to the Lake Muda Jetty, accommodation, all meals, activities, guides and all government permits. Activities include trekking to a cave, or to a Tualang tree where wild honey bees build their nests, visiting saltlicks, wildlife river cruises, river tubing and, for the four- or five-day packages, time to laze around and simply enjoy the rainforest. All packages have a strong interpretation and education focus. Earth Lodge supports conservation and is active in the protection of Ulu Muda. Additionally, it promotes and supports scientific research through the Ulu Muda Field Research Centre.

The departure point for Ulu Muda is usually either via the state capital, Alor Star (also spelt, Alor Setar), or Penang. Both are easily accessible by air, bus or train. An (inefficient) bus service provides access from Alor Star to Kuala Nerang or Sik from Penang. From these towns, taxis provide a connection to the area. However, do not be surprised if the taxi drivers are not familiar with Lake Muda (or Tasik Muda). You can help them by using navigation apps like Waze or Google Map and typing 'Lake Muda Jetty'. Alternatively, rent a car and drive. Due to the difficulty of getting to Lake Muda, Earth Lodge can help arrange road transfers from George Town, Butterworth, Sungai Petani or Alor Star.

The other option is Muda Resort, operated by Muda Agricultural Development Agency (MADA), a federal government agency that manages the three dams. Just 3km (1.9 miles) from the jetty, it offers comfortable duplex chalets with air conditioning and hot water, basic rooms with two or four beds, or basic dorms. The resort was built in the 1960s as accommodation for engineers building the dams and has a swimming pool. However, bookings can be difficult as it is popular with government agencies, especially during weekends and holidays. Small groups or single travellers need to walk out to roadside stalls for meals as the restaurant only caters to larger groups.

Stay in comfortable park accommodation

Perlis

The northwestern states of Perlis and Kedah form the border with Thailand and offer several fascinating destinations to explore from Langkawi. Both states are accessible from Langkawi by ferry to either Kuala Perlis (Perlis) or Kuala Kedah (Kedah). Various road and rail border crossings make it easy to travel between Malaysia and Thailand.

The north-west peninsula is best explored by car as air and rail connections are limited. It is possible to hire a car in Kangar for exploring Perlis and southern Thailand (rental firms can advise on taking Malaysian registered cars across the border and back again).

Perlis is Malaysia's smallest state

Cool off in a stream at Kaki Bukit

at 821km² (319mi²) and the only one without an airport. Most people travel along the North South Highway or via train into Arau. The main road crossing into Thailand is at Bukit Kayu Hitam in Kedah while for train travellers, it is Padang Besar (also a road crossing). There is, however, a small border crossing at Wang Kelian (Perlis) and Wang Prachan (Thailand) that provides an alternative route for those travelling by road between Perlis and southern Thailand.

From Langkawi, Kuala Perlis is the closest arrival port on the mainland and its docks bustle with activity as deep-sea boats return with their catch. This small fishing town at the mouth of the Perlis River is well known for its delicious seafood restaurants. However, no dish is more popular here, and in many parts of the Perlis, than *laksa* (there are many versions throughout Malaysia but it is *Perlis laksa* they slurp down here).

The royal town of Arau, located close to Kangar, is small with several distinctive buildings in the town centre. The Royal Palace (Istana Arau) is a stately building situated opposite the large Royal Mosque. The train station is just behind the Royal Mosque.

Both Perlis and Kedah are known as Malaysia's rice bowl states. During the growing season, the flat landscape covering both states is a sea of green rice stems swaying gently in the wind, which just prior to harvesting, change to golden yellow.

The land is rarely bare and then only briefly when it is being prepared for another crop. It is planted with two rice crops annually and, for many villagers, their daily lives are determined by the rice growing cycle. Mechanization has replaced many of the labour-intensive agricultural practices supplanting the buffaloes, which nevertheless can still be seen in the Perlis countryside.

Kaki Bukit, a small tin mining town that thrived in the 1970s and 1980s is worth visiting. Here, the area around Gua Kelam cave is a popular riverine recreational area that gets crowded at the weekends as well as school and public holidays. A stream flows from the 370m (1,213ft)-long cave; locals love to bathe in the river and picnic along its banks. It is possible to walk the length of the cave along a raised wooden path and exit in the Wang Tangga valley which leads to the remote village of Wang Kelian some distance away.

Further north, Perlis State Park (PSP) forms the western border between Peninsular Malaysia and Thailand. It was planned as a trans-frontier conservation project between the two countries with PSP and Thailand's Thale Ban (or Thaleban) National Park (p.156) but this did not materialize. However, they adjoin each other to provide an extensive protected ecological habitat. The 4,380 ha (10,823 acre)-park is located in Wang Mu and Mata Ayer Forest Reserves along the Nakawan Range which at 38km (23.6 miles) is Malaysia's longest continuous stretch of limestone hills (the range also continues into southern Thailand). The range supports semi-deciduous forest that is home to some unique flora and fauna some of which is endemic to the area.

Cliff Cycad (*Cycas clivicola*) which only grows in Perlis, Langkawi, Perak and parts of southern Thailand is widely distributed over the limestone hills of PSP. This species of cycad is a living fossil that botanists estimate to be over 250 million years old (p.136).

More than 60 mammal species have been recorded including the Stump-tailed Macaque (*Macaca arctoides*), which is a vulnerable and a rarely seen species in Malaysia. Other noted species are the White-handed Gibbon (*Hylobates lar*), Dusky Leaf Monkey (*Trachypithecus obscurus*), Black Panther (*Panthera pardus*) and Crab-eating Mongoose (*Herpestes urva*). The park is also home to 32 bats, 211 birds (including six hornbills) and 46 reptile species.

Life at the Wang Kelian border crossing just outside the park couldn't be any sleepier. It once had a vibrant cross-border Sunday market with stalls around the Customs and Immigration facilities but this has closed.

Other nature-based sites in Perlis include Lake Melati (just north of Kangar), Bukit Ayer Recreational Park (at Sungai Batu Pahat) and the adjacent Snake and Reptile Farm housing 20 snake species. This centre conducts research on these snakes and their venom, and is open to the public.

Where to Stay

Visitors soon realise they are in an isolated part of the world when they try to locate and book accommodation. There are no options in Perlis State Park, Kaki Bukit is the closest accommodation on the Malaysian side of the border. This is only homestay (like an English bed and breakfast with a private room in a family home). Duk D'Kampung Villagestay (T: +60 19 454-3555) is a possibility. Other than that, visitors will have to stay in either Padang Besar or Kangar both some distance from the park. The best option is in neighbouring Thailand at Thale Ban National Park (p.156).

Thale Ban National Park

The entrance to Thale Ban National Park is just a few kilometres north of the Wang Kelian border crossing. Declared in 1980, it covers an area of 198km^2 (75.7mi^2) and is some 1,000km (386 miles) from the Thai capital, Bangkok.

Perlis State Park is closer to Thale Ban than it to the Perlis state capital of Kangar and it is easier to stay here while visiting the far north of Perlis. Accommodation is offered in basic but clean chalets and there is a lakeside restaurant.

While the landscape is similar to PSP, the accessible lake within a valley near park headquarters in Thale Ban makes the park quite unique (the lakes within PSP are not as accessible). There are even mangrove species in the western side of the park but it is the lotus-lined lake that makes Thale Ban so picturesque. A wooden boardwalk provides access to the freshwater lake, which can be very colourful when the pink lotus flowers are in full bloom.

Steep limestone cliffs frame the valley and further inland there are several caves. Chin Mountain at 756m (2,480ft) is the highest peak in the park. The mountain

Admire lotus-lined lakes

shares the border with Malaysia making it also the northern-most point in Peninsular Malaysia and the highest peak in PSP. The foothills of the mountain are mostly covered in lowland tropical forest and mixed deciduous forest (the latter is unusual in the region) while near the peak, hill dipterocarp forest flourishes.

The bird and animal life is as varied as in neighbouring Perlis. The park is popular with birdwatchers who travel here to see, among other species, Yellow Bittern (*Ixobrychus sinensis*), Oriental Honey Buzzard (*Pernis ptilorhynchus*), barbets, flycatchers, swifts, swallows, owls and herons.

Where to Stay

Booking accommodation in a Thai national park is problematic for those who don't speak or read Thai. While there are chalets in Thale Ban National Park, pre-booking one is challenging. Visitors could try their luck or choose to stay just north of the park near Wang Prachan. Wangprachan Organic Homestay and Café (T: +66 89 469-9206) is good for food and comfortable accommodation just a few kilometres from the park.

Spot the Yellow Bittern amongst reeds

Koh Tarutao Marine National Park

Located in Satun Province, the 50 islands in and near the 152km² (58.7mi²) Koh Tarutao Marine National Park have captured the attention of intrepid young travellers. Best accessed during the dry season (November to May), the main tourist islands are Koh Lipe and Koh Adang with boats departing from the mainland port of Pak Bara (there is also a service from Langkawi, mostly from October to May). Koh Lipe is developed with chalets, Adang to the north is densely forested with white-sand beaches and is especially popular as a day visit for snorkellers.

Sea gypsies (known as *chow lair* or *chow leh* in Thailand) have lived in the area for centuries but now they share the beautiful beaches and emerald water with tourists seeking an isolated paradise. Beaches on Lipe such as Sunrise and Hat Pattaya are now lined by mostly low-key chalet and bungalow accommodation. Sunset Beach is the least developed of all the three beaches.

While both islands have been well and truly discovered, they still remain free from large development so far probably because of their isolation and relative difficulty of access.

The wider Tarutao National Park is a place to relax as there are few

Relax on Koh Lipe in the Andaman Sea

developments and attractions apart from snorkelling and diving. However, many places close in the low season (mid-May to mid-November) because of the monsoon and access to some islands in the marine park can be problematic.

Where to Stay

There are many choices of resort on Koh Lipe including Cabana Lipe, Koh Lipe Castaway, Mali Sunrise Beach, Serendipity Beach and Wapi.

Koh Adang is mostly untouched

Index

Acknowledgements

While many people contributed to this book, specific thanks are extended to Andy Yow Sing Lai (Rebak Island Resort Langkawi), David Bradley (Sunset Valley Holiday Houses), Beverley Hon (Xcess Communication), Hymeir Kamarudin (Earth Lodge), Narelle McMurtrie (Bon Ton Resort), Anthony Wong (Frangipani Langkawi Resort and Spa), Reginald Pereira (Tanjung Rhu Resort), Zoher Mustan (Tanjung Rhu Resort) and Mohd Os Effendi (Darulaman Sanctuary).

First published in the United Kingdom in 2022 by John Beaufoy Publishing Ltd
11 Blenheim Court, 316 Woodstock Road, Oxford OX2 7NS, England
www.johnbeaufoy.com

10 9 8 / 6 5 4 3 2 1

Photo Credits

L: left, R: right, T: top, B: bottom, M: middle
All photographs by David Bowden except:
Nick Baker 102B, 103T, 118M, 119B, 121B, 124M, 126T; Berjaya Resorts 45; Shutterstock/Marius
Dobilas 90; Mohd Ros Effendi 108T, 108M, 110T, 113M, 115B, 119M; Flickr/Tareq Uddin Ahmed 111T
Thomas Brown 125B, Anthony Cramp 100M, Bernard Dupont 120B, 122B, Rushenb 105B, 123T,
123B, 124T, 125T, Dominic Sherony 107M, Bernard Spragg 108T, Jason Thompson 113T, Tontantrave
121M, 124B, Francesco Veronesi 109B, Warrenski 127M; Gan Cheong Weei 129M, 129B, 130M,
131T, 131M, 133T; Graeme Guy 100B, 101M, 103M, 103B, 107T, 107B, 111B, 113B, 115M, 117M,
127B; David Hogan 21, 22, 23, 49, 50T, 68T, 69M, 78, 79, 80–81, 82, 83, 84, 85, 86, 87, 88, 89, 90, 91,
93T, 94, 95, 96, 97; Hymeir Kamarudin 152, 153; Irshad Mobarak 14; Neoh Hor Kee 114T, 114M, 116T
116B; Pelangi Beach Resort 4–5; Pixabay/Erik Karits 104M, Vinson Tan 105M; Evan Quah 122T; Reba
Island Resort 76T; Resorts World Langkawi 29; Tom Reynolds 112B, 116M, 127T, 129T, 136T, 137T;
The St Regis Langkawi 63; The Datai 3T, 7B; Umgawa Zipline 41, 43T; Wikipedia/Shubham Chatterjee
126B, Wibowo Djatmiko 118T, 123M, J. M. Garg 105T, 109T, 120M, Dr Raju Kasambe 120T, Varun
Omanakuttan 109M, Phuentsho 104B, Pawar Pooja 112T, Vengolis 121T.

Great care has been taken to maintain the accuracy of the information contained in this work.
However, neither the publishers nor the authors can be held responsible for any consequences
arising from the use of the information contained therein.

ISBN 978-1-912081-46-2

Edited by Krystyna Mayer
Designed by Gulmohur Press, New Delhi
Project management by Rosemary Wilkinson

Printed and bound in Malaysia by Times Offset (M) Sdn. Bhd.